TS Trains

Yorkshire and the Dales

Contents

About the book

It only seems like yesterday when I went out to check out the locations for the first book. But now almost year later we are on number four. This time we visit the area of Yorkshire centred around Leeds which offers a wide range of traffic. The area used to echo to the sound of Class 56s on long rakes of HAA MGR trains, Class 45s on Trans Pennine Expresses, Class 76s on the long removed Woodhead Route and Deltics thrashing up the East Coast Main Line. But now the area rings to the sound of the 125mph Class 91s and 180s speeding up and down the East Coast Main Line to the sedate pace of the Harrogate loop with Sprinters and Pacers doing the hard work. Not forgetting the power station traffic around the Knottingley area, the stone from Rylstone and Manchester's refuse trains. Such a variation in such a small space. Thanks to all of the family for putting up with a year of my slaving away late into the night over the computer.

Marcus Dawson
September 2010, Hertfordshire

HOW DOES THE BOOK WORK?

Chapter Information

Gives information about the traffic flows for the section of line covered. However, these are subject to change without notice and should be used as a guide only (especially freight workings).

Location Notes

Gives general information about the area - the surroundings, the amount of road traffic, the type of people likely to be encountered, whether wellies will be needed.

Public Transport

Since not everyone has a car, these notes give information on using public transport.
All public transport information is correct at the time of writing. Walking times are given as a guide only.
Bus services and frequencies shown apply to Monday to Friday daytimes only. Weekend and evening services may be different or non existent.

Bus routes and times can change at short notice so please always check before travelling.
Recommended public transport planning tools are:
http://www.northyorkstravel.info
http://www.nationalrail.co.uk/   http://www.transportdirect.info/
http://www.taxiregister.com/   or you can telephone Traveline on 0871 200 2233.
The destination bus stop, where noted, is indicated by a Ⓑ

Amenities

Gives information on toilets, places to eat and other local facilities that can be reached easily from the location.

Accommodation

Gives information on places to stay nearby, if any.

Photographic Notes

Gives information on the times of day* that provide the best light conditions, the height of the bridge parapet, whether a step ladder be useful, whether there is enough room to stand and for a video tripod. What sources of noise would interfere with audio recordings.
Each picture contains details of the time, month and lens so the photographer can plan ahead. In order to make this book, each location has been revisited and checked within the last 2 months and the pictures are representative of the current shot available. If there are any changes they have been noted in the text. All photos were taken by Marcus Dawson unless otherwise stated.
It should also be noted that trees and bushes often encroach on the view during the summer and shots taken in March may not be available in July due to vegetation growth.

Any times quoted represent the summer months when the sun rises early and sets in the late evening. These should be taken as a guide as the sun will rise or set outside these times during certain months of year.

Postcode: X00 0XX   **Lat N00:00:00**   **Long W00:00:00**

Sat Nav information and Road directions

The postcode provides a reference for your Satellite Navigation system. This will take you to the place indicated by the Ⓖ on the map which will be close to the location. If it is not on the location, use the map or the last few yards. These post codes did not include house numbers so if a house number is requested, please ignore it. They were checked using a 2010 Garmin Nuvi system. Other systems should provide similar results.

The location is always at the centre of the map and the Latitude and Longitude provide an absolute reference to this point.

The map squares represent a 1 kilometre scale, which is approximately 2/3rds of a mile.

Acknowledgements

This book would not have been possible without help and original input from:

Mark Allatt, Richard Armstrong, Warren Armstrong, Mark Bearton, Stephen Bersey, Paul Bigland, Scott Borthwick, Peter Bradshaw, Nathan Bridge, Darren Brooks, Ross Byers, Ken Carr, Ron Carr, Alexander Clark, Nigel Cockburn, Albert Dawson, David Dawson, Peter Foster, Marcus Fudge, Neil Gibson, Joan Green, Robert Green, Neil Harvey, 'The HMPS', Steve Jackson, Peter Kellett, Geoff Kerr, Julie Knowles, Lee, Marshall, Andy Mason, Phil Mason, David Maxey, Pauline McKenna, Michael McNicholas, Matthew Moore, Jim Murphy, Kerry Parker, Adam Parkinson, Scott Patterson, Andrew Pearson, John Mac Pherson, Sarah Power, Phil Precious, Bevan Price, John Rinder, Brian Russell, David Russell, James Skoyles, David Smith, Roger Sutcliffe, Mike Taylor, Rob Terrace, Chris Throp, John Turner, Andrew Wade, Mark Walker, Tim Ward, Andrew Wills, Phil Wright.

Important Note

Advice about the general environment of each location is given on each page. This information is a guide only. Always be careful. Avoid leaving your property on display and be aware of your surroundings at all times. There are, sadly, people who will not think twice about trying to steal your equipment.

ECML Doncaster to York and Leeds

General Notes

The line is two track after Doncaster, reverting to four tracks between Colton Junction and York. It is electrified with 25kv overhead lines along its entire length. The general topography of the land is flat, but with the odd small hill.

Passenger Traffic

A number of companies operate services along this stretch of line. The predominant long-distance operator is East Coast, with Class 91s and HSTs. Grand Central operates a small fleet of HSTs and Class 180s. Hull Trains operates Class 180s on the southern half, and Cross Country operates its Voyagers. Local services are provided by Northern Rail and First, using a mixture of Class 158s, 170s and 185s.

Freight Traffic

Slower freight tends to criss-cross the main line to make way for the 125mph trains. Coal, oil, steel and intermodal traffic feeds from the oil terminal at Immingham, the steel works at Scunthorpe and the Europort at Wakefield to destinations around the country.

Occasional Traffic

There is regular charter activity along the line with tours heading from London and the south-east to Tyneside or Scotland. These are usually Class 90- or Class 67-hauled. Doncaster Belmont Yard often produces engineers trains heading to various parts of the east coast. The New Measurement Train is a regular visitor and appears a number of times during the week. There are also a number of stock moves between places such as Wabtec Works in Doncaster and the depots at Heaton (Newcastle) and Neville Hill (Leeds).

1) 180112 heads north on the initial delivery run to Heaton.
Photo by Warren Armstrong, July, 17:45, 50mm

2) 60040 heads through Bishops Wood with an oil train.
Photo by James Skoyles, January, 13:15, 115mm

3) 31459 top & tails with 31602 on a Doncaster circular test train.
Photo by Mark Allatt, March, 13:45, 110mm

ECML Doncaster to York and Leeds

Locations

Ts	8	Askham Bar
Ts	10	Copmanthorpe
Ts	12	Colton Junction
Ts	14	Bishops Wood
Ts	16	Burn
Ts	18	Great Heck
Ts	20	Fenwick
Ts	22	Joan Croft Junc.
Ts	24	Hampole
Ts	26	Wrenthorpe

Askham Bar

Location Notes

A section of fields on the outskirts of York. Some of the fields are often used for livestock so please be careful and respectful of the area.

1) 66213 heads south with a Redcar to Santon iron ore working.
Photo by Phil Precious, April, 11:45, 100mm

Public Transport

There is the York Park and Ride bus service just to the east of the location. This runs, at 15 minute intervals, from stop 'G' outside York Railway Station.

Amenities

Across the road is a large Tesco store with a cafe and toilets.

Accommodation

There is a collection of hotels and guest houses on Tadcaster Road just to the north of the Park and Ride. Being close to York Racecourse expect them to be busy at weekends

Photographic Notes

2) 43014/013 head north to Heaton on the ECML Patrol run.
Photo by Phil Precious, April, 10:45, 100mm

There are options from both sides of the lines but access from one to the other is not immediate and requires a long walk around the fields. However, the location will offer the photographer options for most of the day. The area is mainly fields so will be boggy after rainfall.

For videographers there is plenty of room for tripods but there will be a constant, but faint, background noise from the nearby A64 and other roads.

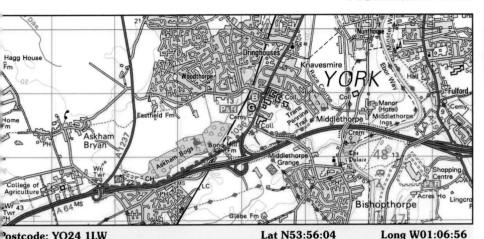

Postcode: YO24 1LW   **Lat N53:56:04**   **Long W01:06:56**

Road Directions

From the York ring road: Head to the south west side of York and follow signs towards the Askham Bar Park and Ride. Follow the A64, in either the east or westbound direction and take the exit signed 'Copmanthorpe/Bishopthorpe and Askham Park and Ride'. Follow the road into York and park either in Tesco's car park or at the Park and Ride.

From the car park walk out and over the railway on Moor Lane from where you will see the field. There is also an alternative car park at the Nature Reserve just off the A1036 which is the eastbound A64 exit. This would be closer to the morning side shot.

3) Mainline Blue 60011 heads south towards Colton Junction with returning tank empties from Jarrow to Lindsey.
   Photo by David Smith, June, 19:00, 50mm

Copmanthorpe

Location Notes
A length of road leading to a rural road crossing over the line. The crossing is mainly used by dog walkers and leads to 'private' land so the crossing gates are usually locked.

1) From the roadside, nearer the road bridge 221138 heads south towards Doncaster with a Cross Country service.
Photo by David Smith, June, 13:39, 50mm

Public Transport
First York, Service 13a, operates at roughly half hourly intervals during the day between York Railway Station and Copmanthorpe Station Road. From there it is about a mile walk to the location.

Amenities
There is nothing at the location but there are a number of shops and pubs back in the village.

Accommodation
There is a Travelodge at the A64 Junction in Colton.

Photographic Notes
The main location is the foot crossing that offers long straight views in both directions. Shots from all sides are constrained by the Overhead Line Equipment, meaning either a head-on shot or more side-on fitting between the masts. However, the crossing and gates are at an angle to the line so there is some scope to get inside the masts.

2) 66149 heads north past the crossing with steel coils.
July, 10:00, 160mm

The area is very quiet so there is little to interfere with audio recordings.

Copmanthorpe

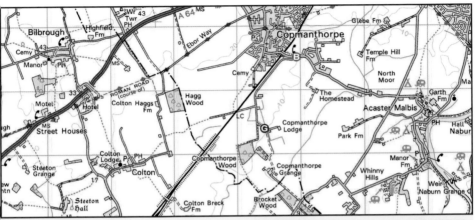

Postcode: YO23 3TL **Lat N53:54:15** **Long W01:08:58**

Road Directions

From the A64, to the south west of York, come off at the exit signed 'York (North) A1237 Harrogate (A59)'
If you are travelling eastbound you will have to follow the signs back to the A64 in the other direction.
Once you cross over the A64 bridge take the left turn (Manor Heath) towards Copmanthorpe, or if you
came off westbound it is the first right. Continue through Copmanthorpe village, you will reach a T-junction
with some shops opposite. Turn right and follow this road, following the signs towards Bishopthorpe and
Acaster Malbis, until you cross the railway. After the bridge there is a right turn, down a 'no through road'.
Follow this road. You can either shoot from the bank near the plant compound or continue down the lane.
Just after the road heads away from the railway there is a right turn that leads to the crossing.
Since the crossing is locked shut you can park up by the gates, or if it is busy, on the verges on the lane.

3) Eurostar double set 3302 & 3304 head south over the crossing with an afternoon working to London.
Photo by Neil Harvey, May, 19:15:, 115mm

Colton Junction

Location notes

About 8 miles south of York and a mile south of Copmanthorpe. This is just south of the junction where the ECML and the line towards Leeds or Knottingley separate. The electrified ECML is to the south and the Leeds lines to the north. Anything heading south out of York will pass the location on one of the lines.

1) 70005 snakes across the trackwork while heading north towards York with coal empties for Holgate Yard.
Photo by David Smith, August, 07:00, 65mm

Public Transport

Harrogate Travel, Service 21, operates an hourly service from York Railway Station to Colton Grange Farm. The journey takes about an hour and it is then about a mile walk to the location.

Amenities

Back at the A64 junction there is a fish and chip shop, a McDonalds Drive-Thru and a petrol station.

Accommodation

There is a Travelodge at the A64 Junction.

Photographic notes

The favoured shots here are morning views of the line to Leeds; changing to the East Coast Main Line in the afternoon to early evening. The lineside is relatively clear from obstructions in all directions with options on all lines for most of the day. The shot of the Leeds lines is a little restricted from the north west side of the line in both directions.

For the view over the bridge sides you might require a step ladder but this will provide you with head-on shots. There is no need for a step ladder at any of the other positions along the roadside.

There is plenty of room around the car parking area for tripods and other than passing traffic. There is little in the way of noise to interfere with audio recordings.

2) 47805 drags 390043 to the site of the NRM Railfest.
Photo by Albert Dawson, May, 16:15, 50mm

3) 60017 heads south down the Church Fenton line.
Photo by Scott Patterson, January, 12:00, 75mm

Colton Junction

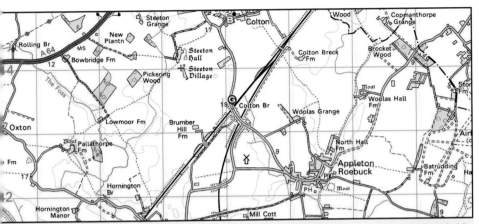

Postcode: YO23 7DU   **Lat N53:52:58**   **Long W01:10:40**

Road directions

From the A64 at Bilbrough Services head east, following the signs for Colton until the 'Colton ¼ mile' left turn. Continue along this road (Colton Lane/Braegate Lane) and you will reach the location.

There is roadside parking at the location but, being a popular location, it can sometimes get crowded. If the main off-road section is full there is plenty of room down the side roads that head south from the location towards Bolton Percy.

4) 66113 catches the setting sun as it hauls 92009 and a diverted Mossend to Daventry working south towards Doncaster.
Photo by Ross Byers, April, 18:00, 90mm

Bishops Wood

Location Notes

A road bridge over the line. To the east is a large wood and open farmland to the west.

1) From the field looking towards the bridge. 55019 speeds north with a Deltic Preservation Society charter to Edinburgh.
Photo by Neil Harvey, April, 10:15, 55mm

Public Transport

Arriva, Services 402/403 operate at half hourly intervals between Leeds Bus Station and Selby. This calls at Thorpe Willoughby from where it would be about a 4 mile walk to the location.

Amenities

There is nothing at the location, but the town of Selby is only a short drive away.

Accommodation

There are a couple of campsites, Sclam Park as mentioned in the road directions, nearby. Failing that Selby has a number of hotels and B&Bs.

Photographic Notes

The line runs almost directly south to the location, with a curve just before the bridge. This provides well lit shots of southbound workings from mid morning onwards.

2) 158859 heads north with a local working.
July, 20:00, 280mm

For northbound workings the line is on a curve and is better suited to late afternoon workings from the bridge or early morning shots from the field.

Shots from the eastern side of the line are hindered by the Bishops Woods themselves and the OLE masts. The location is quiet, apart from passing road traffic. Shots of northbound workings might benefit from a step ladder as you need to shoot over the bridge sides which are about chin height. A step ladder will not be necessary for southbound shots as you do not shoot these from the bridge.

Bishops Wood

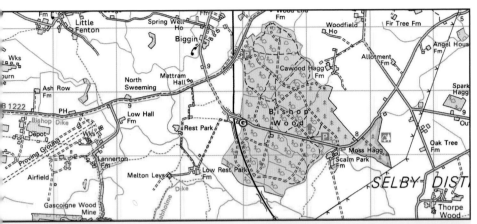

Postcode: LS25 6HN   **Lat N53:47:46**   **Long W01:10:08**

Road Directions

From the south: Leave the A1(M) at Junction 42, signed A63 Leeds, Selby and follow the A63 towards Leeds. After a mile or so take the B1222 exit right to Sherburn in Elmet and follow this road, for about 6 miles, through Sherburn.

From the north: From the A64 York ring road take the exit for the A19, signed to York (Centre) and Selby and keep in the exit's right hand lane following the signs North towards York. Take the first left onto the B1222 (Naburn Lane) towards Sherburn in Elmet for about 10 miles.

When you reach a cross roads with a road off, heading south, to Selby and 'Scalm Park' take it. This road leads to the location. There is a turning just to the West of the bridge where you can park.

3) Easy work on load 5 for 43068 leading a Grand Central working from Sunderland to London King's Cross.
Photo by Andy Mason, June, 14:30, 60mm

Top House Farm, Burn

Location Notes

A popular southbound embankment shot on a dead end lane to a farm. Popular with joggers and dog walkers the area is very quiet and peaceful.

1) 67026 drags a late-running Wakefield Kirkgate to London King's Cross diverted working.
Photo by Neil Gibson, May, 17:00, 0mm

Public Transport

Arriva Yorkshire, Service 405, operates hourly between Selby Bus Station and Doncaster Interchange and passes through the village from where it would be about a mile to walk to the location.

Amenities

There is the Wheatsheaf Pub in the village, but for anything else Selby is a short drive up the road.

Accommodation

There is nothing in the immediate area but Selby has a range of hotels and B&Bs.

Photographic Notes

Primarily a southbound shot, from the middle of the morning until the early evening, there is a range of angles from the bridge and the embankment leading up to it. In the late evenings the sun will come round and provide a northbound shot.

The road is very quite and has plenty of room to stand so it would be ideal for videographers.

2) 90021 heads north on an empty footex to Tyne Yard.
Photo by Neil Gibson, May, 18:15, 85mm

Top House Farm, Burn

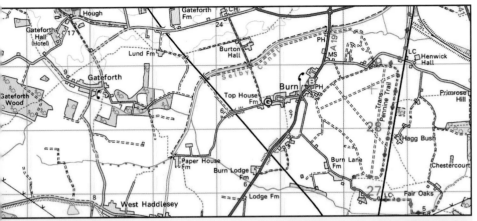

Postcode: YO8 8LR   Lat N53:44:51   Long W01:07:04

Road Directions

From the M62, Junction 34: Take the A19 north towards Selby and Doncaster for about 3 miles. Shortly after crossing the East Coast Main Line you will arrive in the village of Burn. Take the first left into West Lane which will lead you to the location.

The road is sparsely used by motor vehicles so the verges can be used for parking but it would be best to park either off the main bridge area, or on the bridge itself as it is a blind summit and drivers may not be expecting cars on the roadside.

3) With a friendly wave from an East Coast professional, 43295 heads south with an Aberdeen to London working.
   Photo by Richard Armstrong, February, 13:00, 75mm

Great Heck

Location Notes

A pair of shots from either a road bridge or a field to the west of the line opposite the Plasmor Works.

1) 66714 heads north with a gypsum flow from Cottam power station to Newbiggin.
Photo by Neil Harvey, July, 12:45, 60mm

Public Transport

The location is about 1½ miles walk from Hensall Railway Station.

Amenities

There is the Bay Horse Pub and Old Mill Brewery, but the village is without shops. The nearest amenities are in Snaith or Eggborough.

Photographic Notes

The main road bridge offers shots in either direction from the eastern side of the line. The western side of the line is dominated by trees. The south facing shot is taken through a gap in the trees from the pavement. The north facing shot is from the roadside, but there is no pavement. It is possible to stand on the crash barrier or on the fence and lean on a telegraph pole and be off the road. However, for this reason it would be unsuitable for setting up video tripods.

2) An HST speeds north past the Plasmor shunter.
July, 17:45, 130mm

The field shot, to the north of the main road bridge, offers views in both directions from the west of the line and the access road bridge to the Plasmor Works offers a view from the eastern side of the line. However, both positions will suffer from noise from the nearby works.

Great Heck

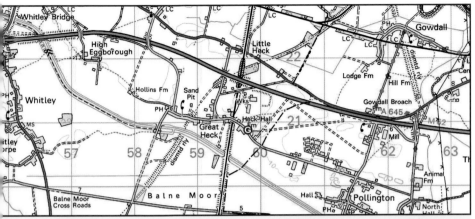

Postcode: DN14 0BB   **Lat N53:40:57**   **Long W01:05:58**

Road Directions

From the M62, Junction 34: Take the A19 towards Selby and York and at the first roundabout take the A645 towards Goole. After about 2 miles, turn right on Long Lane towards Great Heck. Follow this road down and after passing under the M62 there is a turning on the left to the Plasmor Works. You can drive down here and walk to the field location. For the bridge continue down the road, keeping left and you will pass over the bridge. Shortly after the bridge there is a lay-by on the left where you can park.

3) 60093 heads south with an empty steel train to be refilled with coils at the plant in Scunthorpe.
Photo by Darren Brooks, May, 17:30, 125mm

Fenwick

Location Notes
A small staff operated level crossing on a quiet country road.

1) 60015 rumbles towards the crossing with a Leeds to Lindsey oil train.
Photo by Neil Harvey, August, 15:30, 70mm

Public Transport
Wilfreda Beehive, Service 89, provides a sparse service between Doncaster Interchange and Shaw Lane in Fenwick.

Amenities
The Baxters Arms is a short distance, east, down the road from the location.

Accommodation
There is nothing at the location, the nearest options are in the town of Askern to the south west.

Photographic Notes
The crossing and surrounding paths and roadways offer some open views for southbound workings. The crossing gates themselves are just inside the OLE masts allowing for telephoto shots up the line.

There is a small house on the corner of the crossing that makes shots of northbound workings very tight. Being a manned crossing there are no warbling sirens so the crossing itself is quiet but when the gates are closed there may be traffic queuing creating unwanted noise. Freight will often be running slowly at this location having come off the junction at Joan Croft a few miles to the south.

2) 60040 heads south with empty tanks for Lindsey refinery.
Photo by Rob Terrace, August, 19:00, 380mm

3) Eurostar sets 3309/3310 power north to York
Photo by Neil Harvey, August, 14:30, 55mm

Fenwick

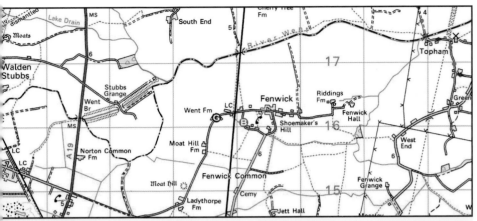

Postcode: DN6 0EZ   **Lat N53:38:21**   **Long W01:06:35**

Road Directions

From the M18, Junction 6: Follow the signs for the A614 (Thorne) and travel about ½ mile along the road until you see a left turn signed to 'Fishlake, Stainforth and Sykehouse'. Follow this road across the River Don bridge and follow it left to Fishlake Village. Take the second right turn, there is a red post box on the left, and then follow the signs to Moss. Once in Moss continue straight through the village and just before you reach the Moss Road Level Crossing, turn right and continue up this road. Turn left upon entering Fenwick village and follow the road to the location on the left.

There is room to park one or two cars on either side on either verges or lay-bys.

4) 70003 heads the inaugural 'Powerhaul Duck' tour down the ECML towards Doncaster before turning left to Hatfield.
Photo by Steve Jackson, April, 12:30, 110mm

Joan Croft Junction

Location Notes
A small staff operated level crossing where the lines from Immingham, Stainforth and Hull join with the northbound East Coast Main line.

1) 91121 speeds north past the crossing, and waiting enthusiasts, with an East Coast express working to Newcastle.
Photo by Matthew Moore, September, 12:45, 90mm

Public Transport
From Adwick railway station the location is about 4½ miles walk. First, Services 50/50A operate frequently, starting at the Doncaster Interchange and passing Adwick Station. This stops on the Oweston Road which would take a mile off the walk.

Amenities
There are lots of shops and supermarkets in Carcroft, including an Asda.

Accommodation
There is a Travelodge at the junction of the M18 and M180 to the east.

Photographic Notes
The line is running roughly north to south at this point so there should be angles available all day. The primary shots are of southbound workings during the morning and afternoon. Two houses at the crossing prevent shots from the western side of the line, other than tight shots of trains coming off the Stainforth line.

2) 66145 joins the northbound ECML from the Stainforth line.
July, 18:45, 150mm

Workings can often pause on the curve awaiting access to the East Coast Main line and can be seen in the distance. The points will set accordingly. Southbound workings will also, sometimes, pause to the north of the location, awaiting the road east. The curve itself is a slow one and freight using it will not be travelling very quickly. Other than traffic waiting at the crossing there is little noise to interfere with video recordings.

Joan Croft Junction

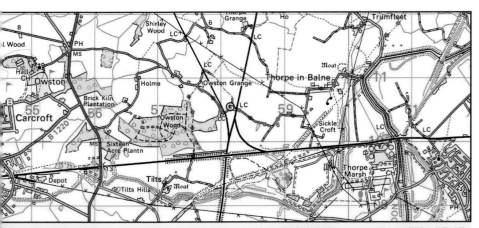

Postcode: DN5 0LU   **Lat N53:35:17**   **Long W01:07:17**

Road Directions

From the M18, Junction 4:Take the A630 west towards Doncaster and at the second roundabout take the 3rd exit (Hatfield Lane) towards Barnby Dun and Hatfield. Once in Barnby Dun there is a junction in front of the 'White Hart' pub, take the left fork and follow this road to the lifting bridge. If you miss the turn you can continue along the main road to reach the bridge. Cross the bridge and immediately after the next river bridge take the right turn towards 'Thorpe and Moss' passing the Thorpe Marsh cooling towers on you left. Carry on up the road and take the left turn signed to 'Thorpe in Baine' continuing through the village and then turn right onto 'Bell Croft Lane' which will lead you to the location.

There is space for a couple of cars on either side of the crossing.

3) Merrily going round from Ferrybridge to Immingham, 66523 returns empties to collect more imported coal..
Photo by Andrew Wills, March, 16:15, 65mm

Hampole

Location Notes
The A1 road overbridge just to the west of the Adwick, Carcroft and Skellow Junctions triangle.

1) 37606 leads an overhead line test train towards Leeds on a tour of Yorkshire with 37602 on the rear.
Photo by Ross Beyers, April, 14:45, 70mm

Public Transport
Adwick Station is served by trains from Doncaster, Leeds, Sheffield and Lincoln.
Arriva Yorkshire, Service 496, operates half hourly from Doncaster Interchange to Red House. This bus also calls at South Elmsall for the Railway Station.

Amenities
Just off the A638 towards Adwick there is a McDonalds Drive-Thru and there is a petrol station just to the north on the A1.

Accommodation
There is a Travelodge on the A1 just to the north of the location.

1) 82212 gets the shove from a 91 towards London.
Photo by Ross Byers, April, 14:45, 70mm

Photographic Notes
The location has been opened up by river bank clearance on the western side of the bridge. You can see for a mile or so in both directions but you will need to stand on tip toes to see over the bridge sides. However you shoot from either side of the main bridge parapet which is protected by a chest high metal bar fence which you can lean on. You are protected, on both sides, by the motorway Armcos but this also means that it is not possible to change direction of shooting, safely, without a long walk back up and down the roadside. The constant stream of traffic makes this location unsuitable for video work.

Hampole

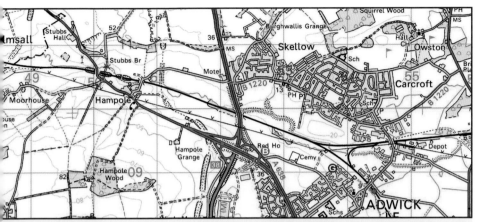

Postcode: DN6 7UW **Lat N53:34:60** **Long W01:12:41**

Road Directions

The location is the A1 overbridge, just to the north of junction 38 where the A1(M) converts back to the plain old A1. There are two options for parking. If you are on the northbound A1 then you can park either on Leys Lane for which the turning is just after the metal footbridge, or in the parking areas around the service areas and Travelodge and then walk back down the path. Option two is take the A638 towards Doncaster, if travelling northbound you will come back under the A1 and come to a roundabout where you will need to take the exit for Adwick Le Street and then back towards the A1(M) southbound. Just after the turning there is a lay-by and grass verge where you can park, this is just after the A1 southbound exit road becomes a two way road.

From here you can walk back up the path on the opposite side to the road to reach the bridge.

3) Napier power back on the ECML. 55022 heads south towards Doncaster and King's Cross with a charter from Preston.
Photo by Andy Mason, June, 07:45, 50mm

Wrenthorpe

Location Notes

A metal footbridge over the line in the middle of housing estates in Wakefield.

1) 45407 heads north towards Leeds with a 'Scarborough Spa Express'.
Photo by Mark Allatt, August, 11:30, 50mm

Public Transport

Arriva, Services 425 and 427, operate frequently between Wakefield Bus Station, which is close to Wakefield Westgate railway station and Bradford Interchange.

Amenities

There is a Chinese takeaway / fish and chip shop on the main road back towards the railway bridge on Bradford Road. There is also a newsagents about a mile south on the Bradford Road.

Accommodation

There are a couple of travel inns off the A650 in Newton Hill.

Photographic Notes

The footbridge has ramps leading up to the bridge offering a range of height options over the line but options from the east of the line are hampered by trees. Given the curve on the track the best options

2) 31459 & 602 on a Doncaster to Doncaster test train.
Photo by Mark Allatt, March, 13:45, 118mm

for the light would be in the afternoon for southbound shots and evenings for northbound.
The area is quiet making it suitable for video work, although bridge vibration may cause problems.

Wrenthorpe

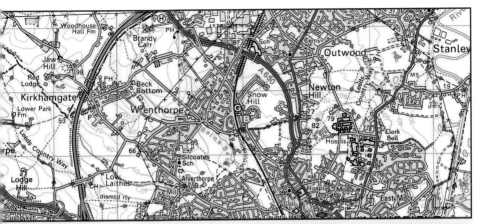

Postcode: WF1 2BP   **Lat N53:41:59**   **Long W01:31:09**

Road Directions

From the M1, Junction 41: Take the A650 south, signed to Wakefield. After entering Wakefield take the first junction off towards Carr Gate and Wrenthorpe. Follow this road (Bradford Road) for about a mile, pass under the railway line and shortly afterwards, take the right turn onto Bowling Avenue where there is an area of hard standing on the right. Either park here, considerately, or use one of the side roads. Off the hard standing is a public footpath that leads to the footbridge.

3) 5690 accelerates away from Westgate station towards Leeds and York with a late-running 'Spa Express'.
   Photo by Mark Allatt, August, 19:40, 32mm

ECML Diversions

General Notes

Although these lines are not used solely as diversionary routes, the chapter covers locations where traffic has been routed off the ECML. Generally the area is open farmland between the urban sprawls of Doncaster, Wakefield and Leeds.

Passenger Traffic

Depending on the area, this is mostly multiple unit traffic. Northern Rail operates most of the local services. Grand Central Class 180s and HSTs are regular users of the route for pathing reasons.

Freight Traffic

The predominant traffic in the area is coal, with trains of DB Schenker, Freightliner and GBRf travelling from collieries and docks to power stations. There are also oil flows from the Humber refineries, intermodal workings from Wakefield Europort, and a sand flow to the glass factory at Monk Bretton.

Occasional Traffic

Scrap trains run on an 'as required' basis. The autumn Rail Head Treatment Trains also cover the area and produce a mixture of traction types operated by DRS and DB Schenker.

1) 180105 heads towards Knottingley past Joan Croft Lane.
Photo by Peter Bradshaw, July, 17:45, 50mm

2) 66842 with a Cardiff Tidal to Stockton empty scrap working.
Photo by Pauline McKenna, July, 18:15, 115mm

3) 67029 passes Welbeck with a Birmingham to York charter.
Photo by Julie Knowles,

ECML Diversions

Locations

Womersley, Post Office Lane LC

Location Notes
A road crossing outside a small village opposite a farm.

1) 180114 heads north with a Grand Central working to Bradford.
Photo by Mark Walker, June, 16:15, 160mm

Public Transport
Arriva Yorkshire, Services 409 and 420, run between Doncaster Interchange and Pontefract Bus Station and call in Wormersley at the roundabout at the end of Station Road.

Amenities
There is nothing in the village, the nearest town is Knottingley to the north west or Askern to the south east.

Photographic Notes
A reasonably tight head-on shot of a long straight towards Knottingley well suited for telephoto lenses. You can use the crossing fence to lean on. In both directions the line is flanked by trees, so shadows will be an issue, but there are breaks to let the sun through.

The crossing is an automatic half barrier so there will be warbling sirens whenever a working is approaching making the location unsuitable for video work.

2) 66194 heads towards Knottingley with an MGR.
Photo by Mark Walker, June, 16:45, 325mm

Womersley, Post Office Lane LC

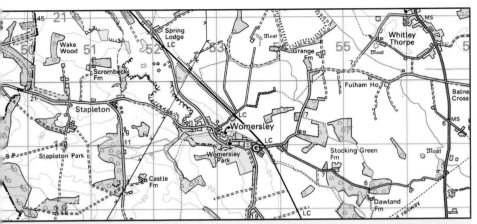

Postcode: DN6 9BL   **Lat N53:39:52**   **Long W01:11:16**

Road Directions

From the M62, Junction 34: Take the A19 south towards Doncaster and continue south for about ¾ mile, passing first the George and Dragon Pub and then 'slow' markings on the road. Take the next right turn onto Gravel Hill Lane and continue along the road for a mile. At the T-junction turn right and continue over the first level crossing into Wormersley village. At the roundabout turn right, following the signs to Darrington. In the village there is a right turn that is marked with a 'Risk of Grounding' signs for lorries. Take this turning (Cow Lane) and follow it until you reach the location.
There are some field entrances where you can park to the east of the crossing.

3) After passing Ferrybridge power station, 180101 heads towards the crossing with a Bradford to London working.
   Photo by Mark Walker, June, 11:45, 325mm

Criddling Stubbs, Spring Lodge LC

Location Notes

A road crossing between two villages with just a former crossing keeper's house in the area.

1) 66728 heads towards Doncaster with a rake of returning coal empties from Drax to Immingham Docks.
Photo by Pauline McKenna, February, 10:15, 105mm

Public Transport

Arriva Yorkshire, Service 420, runs between Doncaster Interchange and Pontefract Bus Station and calls at both Womersley Village and Cridling Stubbs Village from where it would be about a mile walk back to the crossing. The bus route uses the crossing and there also is an unlisted bus stop there.

Amenities

There is nothing in the immediate area, but the town of Knottingley is a short drive to the north.

Accommodation

There is a Travelodge just off Junction 33 of the M62.

2) 66163 heads an empty spoil train towards Doncaster.
Photo by Pauline McKenna, February, 10:15, 105mm

Photographic Notes

The line runs roughly north-west to south-east through the location and is fairly open so it will be free from shadows for most of the day.

The crossing is automatic half barriers so they will warble when a train approaches, making the crossing unsuitable for video. But you do have options from the roadside and the fields around the crossing.

Criddling Stubbs,Spring Lodge LC

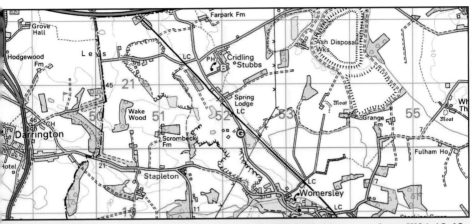

Postcode: DN6 9BB　　　　　**Lat N53:40:44**　　　　　**Long W01:12:42**

Road Directions

From the M62, Junction 34: Take the A19 south towards Doncaster and continue south for about ¼ mile, and as the road curves to the left there is a turning on the right (Whitefield Lane) signed towards Criddling Stubbs. Take this and follow the road for about 3 miles, going around Criddling Stubbs village, turn right at the T junction and almost immediately left into Stubbs Lane. The location is about ¼ mile down the lane. There are a number of lay-bys where you can park around the crossing.

3) 60028 heads towards Knottingley, before travelling on to York with the 'Grid Arising' tour.
Photo by Pauline McKenna, September, 13:30, 105mm

Stourton

Location Notes
A road overbridge between Freightliners Midland Road depot and Stourton intermodal terminal.

1) #2 66844 passes the intermodal terminal with empties from a short-lived Derby to Shipley scrap flow.
Photo by Pauline McKenna, July, 19:30, 105mm

Public Transport
First, Services 85/87, run over the bridge at the location and they depart from the Wellington Street stop which is just outside the Central Station, under The Queens Hotel arch and then to the left.

Amenities
There are two pubs on the A639, as well as a McDonalds Drive-Thru. Further along are some supermarkets.

Accommodation
There are two hotels on the A61 and Leeds City Centre has many hotels.

2) #2 67013 with a Doncaster to Neville Hill Mark III move.
Photo by Pauline McKenna, September, 19:00, 100mm

Photographic Notes
The bridge sides are low enough to lean your elbows on so a step ladder is not required.There is usually some activity either in the yard to the south or the Freightliner depot. There are usually lots of people passing by and other enthusiasts about. There is plenty of traffic on the road which will create noise to interfere with audio recordings, but there is space for tripods for video cameras.

Stourton

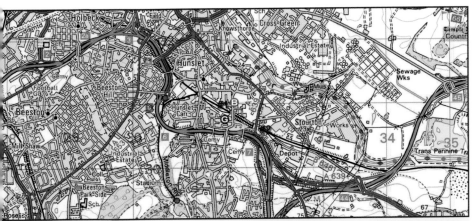

Postcode: LS10 2ER   **Lat N53:46:23**   **Long W01:31:21**

Road Directions

From the M621, Junction 7: Take the Stourton exit and follow the signs up the A61 towards Leeds and Hunslet. Keep in the left hand lane at the traffic lights and follow the road round, you will pass the Crooked Billet pub on the right. At the next set of lights turn left onto Sussex Avenue and follow this road round until you reach the location.

There is plenty of street parking in the area.

3) #1 45407 passes Freightliner's Leeds Midland Road depot while working the 'Scarborough Spa Express'.
Photo by Marcus Fudge, July, 12:00, 160mm

Burn Lane, Temple Hirst

Location Notes

A small staff operated crossing on the Selby diversion route a few miles north of Temple Hirst Junction.

1) 60059 heads north with stone from Peak Forest.
Photo by John Mac Pherson, May, 15:00, 50mm

Public Transport

Arriva Yorkshire, Service 405 operates between Doncaster Interchange and Selby Bus Station and calls in Burn village from where it will be about a mile and a half walk to the location

Amenities

There is nothing in the immediate area, the nearest town is Selby to the north which has a range of shops and supermarkets.

Photographic Notes

There is a single residence opposite the crossing that will block shots of southbound workings in the afternoon and the crossing keeper's portacabin slightly restricts angles of northbound workings but apart from that the area is just open farmland.

2) 66706 approaches the crossing with an Intermodal.
Photo by Andrew Mason, March, 12:45, 40mm

If you are looking south down the line you can see lights approaching that may be ECML traffic which diverges west at Temple Hirst Junction. The location is open countryside, the only extraneous noise is from traffic pausing at the crossing.

Burn Lane, Temple Hirst

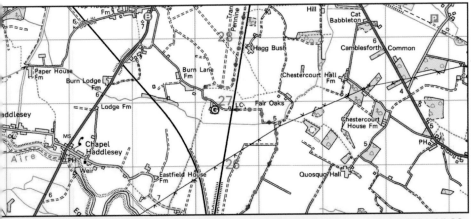

Postcode: YO8 8QJ   **Lat N53:42:45**   **Long W01:05:38**

Road Directions

From the M62, Junction 34: Head north on the A19 towards Selby. You will pass Eggborough Power Station on the way. About ⅓ mile after passing over the East Coast Main Line is a right turn, Brick Kiln Lane. Take this, then the second left (Burn Lane) which you follow to the location.

From the A64, York Ring Road: Take the A19 exit towards Selby and continue along the road past Selby following the A19 signs towards Doncaster. Continue through Burn village and take the left turn into Brick Kiln land and then the next left into Burn Lane, which you follow to the location.

There are spaces for a couple of cars on either side of the crossing.

3) With Temple Hirst Junction in the background and the ECML diverging to the right, 66716 heads to Selby.
Photo by Andrew Mason, June, 07:45, 650mm

Hambleton Junctions

Location Notes

A collection of paths, crossings, both foot and bridge, over the East Coast Main Line and the route from Selby to Leeds. There are also junctions between these lines.

1) 66116 comes off the ECML and heads west with a Felixstowe to Wakefield Europort intermodal.
Photo by Scott Paterson, April, 14:15, 65mm

Public Transport

Arriva Yorkshire, Services 403/402, operate between Selby Bus Station and Leeds Bus Station and call in the village.

Amenities

There is nothing at the location, but there are two pubs in the village.

Accommodation

There is The Owl Hotel in Hambleton village.

Photographic Notes

The main location is to the west of the junctions and involves shots of workings either coming over the flyover from the Selby direction or the East Coast Main Line junction or heading west down a long straight in the eastbound direction.

There is a farmers' track that leads all the way from the west junction and follows the curve to the ECML. On the Selby line there is a large embankment that runs parallel to the line, offering a height advantage over workings.

The whole area is open fields and farmland so it is free from noise and is suitable for video work.

2) 67029 powers east with a management outing.
Photo by Neil Gibson, September, 13:45, 50mm

3) 67002 rejoins the ECML after diverting via Wakefield.
Photo by Scott Patterson, April, 15:15, 55mm

Hambleton Junctions

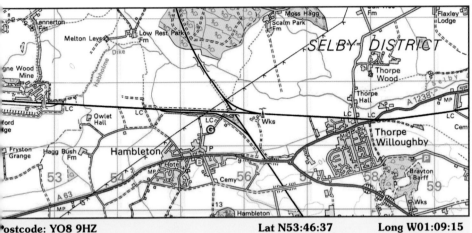

Postcode: YO8 9HZ   **Lat N53:46:37**   **Long W01:09:15**

Road Directions

From the A1(M), Junction 42: Take the A63 east towards Selby for about 5 miles until you reach the village of Hambleton. On the way out of the village, near the Wheatsheaf pub and signed for local traffic, is St Marys Approach on the left. Take this and then turn right into Station Road. Continue up Station Road to the location, or turn right up Scalm Lane for an alternative position.

There is plenty of off road parking at the end of both lanes, but take care not to block any gates or access.

4) Coming off the East Coast Main Line 66706 powers an Immingham to Tyne Dock empty wagon move.
Photo by Scott Patererson, May, 17:00, 45mm

Burton Salmon

Location Notes
A popular road bridge near the junction where the lines from York split to either Leeds or Knottingley.

1) 66414 heads a diverted Tesco working past the cattle dock.
Photo by Andy Mason, March, 09:45, 65mm

Public Transport
Arriva Yorkshire, Services 492 and 493, run from Pontefract, via Knottingley and South Milford and call close to the bridge.

Accommodation
There is nothing in the immediate area. There are some hotels in the Castleford area and there is a Travelodge to the south along the A162 at the Junction with the M62.

Photographic Notes
The shot of southbound workings (facing towards Church Fenton and York) has a wide pavement and will be well lit until early afternoon, the other side of the bridge is narrower, but still usable. Both bridge sides are low and a step ladder is not required. The road traffic noise here may be a problem for videographers.

For the shot from the cattle dock you will need to walk back down Hilliam Lane and double back along the second of the field edges to reach this location. The first field now has no public access, so please do not cross over it.

This is free from traffic noise and would better suit videographers.

2) 6233 heads north towards York.
Photo by Mark Allatt, April, 09:15, 105mm

3) 66140 heads west with coal for Ferrybridge.
Photo by Kerry Parker, March, 14:15, 300mm

Burton Salmon

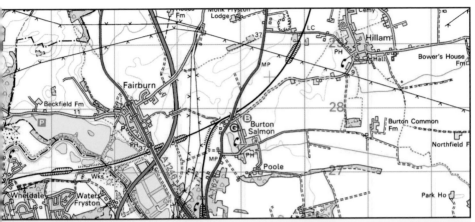

Postcode: LS25 5JQ **Lat N53:44:42** **Long W01:15:37**

Road Directions

From the A1(M), Junction 42: Head east along the A63 for about 2 miles until you reach the roundabout with the A162. Here take the third exit (south) towards Burton Salmon and Brotherton. Follow the A162 until you reach the bridge. Once you have crossed over the bridge Hillam Lane is the first left. There is a grass verge on Ledgate Lane, which is the first right of off Hillam Lane where you can park your car safely.

4) 37059, with 47712 on the back, leads the 'Solway Viking' stock on a turning move from York to York via Leeds.
Photo by Ross Byers, May, 13:45, 90mm

Normanton

Location Notes
A road bridge, on the route to the local recycling centre, high above the lines.

1) 67002 drags a Wakefield Westgate East Coast service because of engineering work on the Doncaster-Wakefield line.
Photo by Scott Patterson, April, 10:15, 45mm

Public Transport
The bridge is just over a mile walk from Normanton Railway Station by road and footpath.

Amenities
There are a few shops around the station in Normanton. Otherwise there is a retail park with fast food outlets just off the A638 in Wakefield to the left just before the railway viaduct.

Accommodation
There are a few small hotels in Normanton, including one opposite the station.

Photographic Notes
The sides of the bridge are high so a step ladder is essential. There are narrow pavements on either side of the road so you will be standing off the road. It is the route into both the local recycling centre and an industrial land fill site so expect lorries passing regularly. The cutting

2) 66719 with a Leeds to Doncaster Decoy wagon move.
Photo by Mark Walker, May, 12:45, 35mm

sides are high but sloped, so shadows will become a problem for southbound workings in the early or late parts of the day when the sun is low.

Normanton

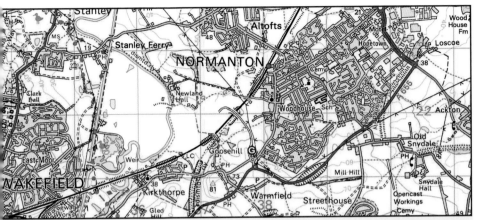

Postcode: WF6 1QG   **Lat N53:41:35**   **Long W01:25:58**

Road Directions

From the M1, Junction 42: Head east on the M62 or from the A1(M), Junction 41, head west on the M62. Then from junction 31, of the M62, take the A655 south and follow the signs towards Wakefield. At the roundabout with the large electricity pylon on the right follow the signs for Welbeck and then for Household waster recycling centre. Follow this road up to the bridge.

Just before the bridge there are grass verges where you can park your car off road. The road is used by heavy lorries from the recycling centre so make sure you leave plenty of room for them to pass.

3) 47501 leads 47712 and the Cargo-D Mark IIIs north east towards Normanton on a Leicester to Carlisle charter.
Photo by Ross Byers, July, 08:30, 95mm

Milford Junction

Location Notes

Also known as Monk Fryston, this is a popular road bridge overlooking the junction of the line towards Hambleton and Selby, with the South Milford sidings behind. The main road to Monk Fryston is behind this bridge so this road is quiet, but traffic approaches from the west round a bend so be wary.

1) A southbound cross-country working from Edinburgh to Plymouth clatters across the junction pointwork.
Photo by Pauline McKenna, March, 11:30, 155mm

Public Transport

Arrivia Yorkshire, Services 492 and 493, operate hourly between Pontefract, Knottingley and South Milford, and Church Fenton railway stations and call in the village.

Amenities

The village has a pub and a post office/village stores

Accommodation

There is the Monk Fryston Hall a few minutes walk from the location, or for a more economical option, there are some Travel Inn type hotels on the A63 to the west.

Photographic Notes

The bridge offers views in both directions with a metal parapet that is roughly chest height, so a step ladder is not required. There is little to throw shadows on the line once the sun is up. The points will give a clue of the direction of the approaching working. The pavement on the northern side of the bridge would not be wide enough for video tripods without obstructing the path. You can however shoot southbound workings from Ingthorpe Lane without blocking the path. Road noise will be a problem, but the road is not very busy.

2) 59206 heads towards Gascoigne Wood to re-load.
Photo by Neil Harvey, July, 16:15, 75mm

Milford Junction

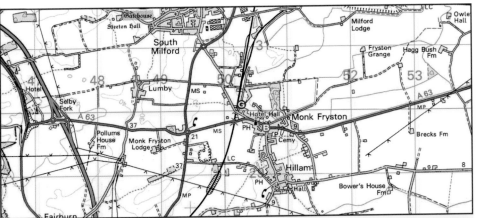

Postcode: LS25 5DD   **Lat N53:45:50**   **Long W01:14:25**

Road Directions

From the A1M, Junction 42: Take the A63 and follow the signs for Selby east for about a mile. You will see the line to your right as you approach the bridge over the line. This is not the bridge you are looking for. Once over the bridge you will enter the village of Monk Fryston. As the main road curves round to the right turn left into Lumby Lane, signed to South Milford. Follow this road for a few hundred yards and you will reach the correct bridge.

There are a couple of parking spaces on Ingthorpe Lane, but please observe the 'Keep Clear' markings. If this area is full then there are options in the streets back in Monk Fryston.

3) The scene has changed little since 1996 when 59206 hauled loaded coal to Drax on a daily basis.
Photo by Neil Harvey, July, 15:00, 75mm

Hare Park Junction

Location Notes

A foot crossing just after the junction where the ECML to Leeds splits off. From here workings can reach Leeds via Normanton, York via Church Fenton or head west towards Healey Mills and Manchester.

1) 66529 shivers south towards the ECML with a Bredbury to Roxby binliner.
Photo by Mark Walker, February, 12:15, 90mm

Public Transport

Arriva Yorkshire, Services 194,195 and 196, run from Wakefield Bus Station passing Kirkgate and Sandal & Agbrigg rail stations and call along the High Street in Crofton village.

Amenities

There is a Sainsburys Local and post office on the High Street in Crofton village.

Accommodation

There is nothing in the village. But there are a number of Travel Inn type hotels on the A636 nearer the M1.

Photographic Notes

The line curves in from the ECML and then continues on a long straight up to Crofton Junction, about a mile away. There are a few lineside trees but nothing major to cast shadows. The shot has well lit options from about 10:00 in the morning until late evening.

The area is quiet and would be well suited to video recordings as workings heading west will be accelerating away from the junction.

2) 60028 restarts a binliner at Hare Park Junction.
Photo by Mark Allatt, June, 13:00, 80mm

Hare Park Junction

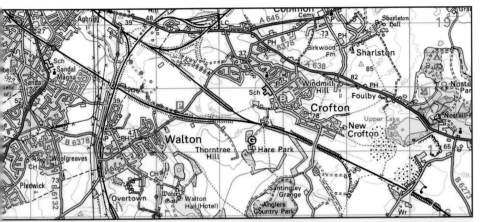

Postcode: WF4 1HT **Lat N53:39:13** **Long W01:26:16**

Road Directions

From the M1, Junction 39: Take the A636 east, signed to Wakefield, and at the second roundabout take the fourth exit, towards Barnsley, on the A6186. The road joins with the A61 and then after about ¼ mile get into the right hand lane, at the traffic lights opposite the Three Horseshoes Pub, and turn right into Carr Lane. Follow this road for about ⅓ mile and turn right into the B6378. Continue along this road now called Walton Station Lane, to the T-junction just after you go under two sets of power lines. Turn right into Greenside (still the B6378) and take the next left turn, signed to 'Waterton Park Hotel' onto Shay Lane, crossing over the line to Monk Bretton. Continue along this road into Crofton Village. You will pass under the ECML and the Kirkgate line. At the T-junction at the end of the road turn right, towards 'Crofton Community Centre' and continue for about ½ mile until you reach a mini roundabout, just after the Sainsburys on the left. Turn right and continue down Hare Park Lane. Park on the roadside just before the road curves to the left and continue on foot. Walk down the farm track and bear left at the farm units, this foot path leads to the foot crossing.

3) 57006 leaves the wires behind and heads towards Normanton with a Cardiff Tidal to Shipley scrap flow.
Photo by Mark Walker, March,17 15:, 35mm

Harrogate Loop

General Notes

Set in the rolling hills of Yorkshire, this 36 mile line is mostly double track but with two short sections of single track between Poppleton and Knaresborough. There are a number of tunnels and viaducts, including the 31-arch Crimple Viaduct to the south of Harrogate.

1) 155343 &153363 branch off to the loop while working the daily shuttle between Leeds and Knaresborough. *July, 13:00, 130mm*

Passenger Traffic

The line is operated by Northern Rail with a number of units shuttling between Leeds and Knaresborough, and some continuing to York. A mixture of Classes 150, 153 and 155 is the staple power.

Freight Traffic

There is no freight traffic booked to use any of the route.

Occasional Traffic

Excursions frequently use the line. The 'Scarborough Spa Express' and the Northern Belle set appear regularly. The route is also used to turn a northbound train from York so it can head south again without the need for a run-round.

The line's low use also means engineers trains are few and far between. Test trains put in the occasional appearance, but are

2) 47712 leads a Harrogate flower show special west. *Photo by Neil Harvey, April, 12:00, 55mm*

usually in transit rather than carrying out testing. The autumn RHTT traffic has recently produced traction from both DRS and DB Schenker.The autumnal RHTT traffic has recently produced traction from both DRS and DB Schenker.

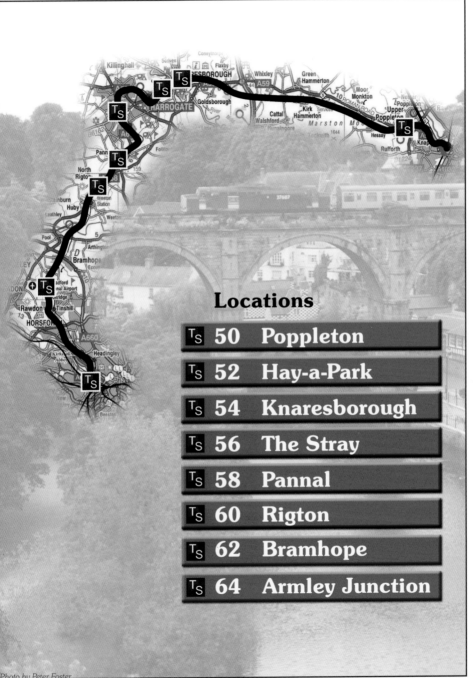

Locations

Photo by Peter Foster

Poppleton

Location Notes
This is a road bridge and surrounding fields, to the west of the station which is the start of the single track section to Hammerton.

1) An unidentified 142 catches the evening sunlight as it ambles west after leaving Poppleton station.
July, 19:15, 95mm

Public Transport
Poppleton station is served by an hourly service from York which continues to Leeds.

Amenities
There is a small village post office and two pubs on Main Street which is a left turn off of Black Dike Lane

Accommodation
The Red Lion pub, on the A59 to the east of Poppleton, offers accommodation or there is a Travel Inn on the Millfield Lane Industrial Estate just off the A1237.

Photographic Notes
The primary shot here is of westbound workings from the bridge. They will usually be accelerating as they have to stop at the station to obtain the token for the single track section to Hammerton. The shot is

2) 37408 tails the Arriva shuttle service to Carlisle.
August, 07:15, 35mm

well lit from late morning, once the sun has come round, until the evening. There are power lines running across the fields that some may find objectionable. Later in the evening a side-on shot is possible from the lane leading off the bridge

The location is on the A59 so traffic noise will be a problem for videographers.

Poppleton

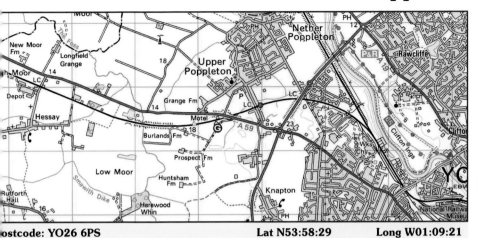

ostcode: YO26 6PS   Lat N53:58:29   Long W01:09:21

oad Directions

rom the A1237 York ring road take the A59 towards Harrogate and Northminster Business Park.
ne location is the A59 road bridge. You can park on the verges on the lane to the west of the bridge.

) 47200 & 828 thrash away from the station after a token exchange with a tour bound for Norwich.
Photo by Mark Bearton, March, 12:45, 135mm

Hay-a-Park Crossing

Location Notes

A gated occupational crossing on a farm track in open fields to the east of Knaresborough.

1) The Royal Train heads away from Knaresborough towards York while on a trip around the Harrogate loop.
Photo by Peter Bradshaw, July, 14:15, 116mm

Public Transport

The location is about 1½ miles, on foot, from Knaresborough Railway station which is well served by trains from both York and Leeds

Amenities

If you follow the lane left, from the north of the crossing, you will reach Chain Lane where there is a fish and chip shop and newsagents.

Accommodation

Knaresborough has a wide range of hotels, but will be busy during the summer as it is a tourist hot spot.

Photographic Notes

The area around the crossing is flat and apart from a few trees and bushes there is little to cast shadows. The line is also straight for a mile or so therefore it is easy to see oncoming workings. The fences for the crossing can offer a height boost.

The area is also very quiet and has no extraneous noise sources, other than the wind, to hinder audio recordings. There is also plenty of room to set up video tripods.

2) 150205 on the to & fro between Leeds and York.
July, 18:15, 130mm

3) 70013 heads east to Scarborough via York.
Photo by Peter Bradshaw, September, 10:00, 135mm

Hay-a-Park Crossing

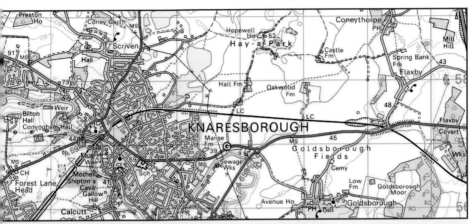

ostcode: HG5 0ST   **Lat N54:00:43**   **Long W01:26:20**

oad Directions

rom the A1237 York ring road take the A59 towards Harrogate and Northminster Business Park. Follow e A59 for about 12 miles until you reach the outskirts of Knaresborough with a brown tourist sign to 'Old other Shiptons's Cave 2 miles'. Follow the A59 into Knaresborough. You will pass a car dealership on e right. Then, about ¼ mile after this, there is a pair of houses on the right and after this is the dirt track lay-A-Park Lane) up to the crossing.

rive up the lane and park your car on one side of the crossing taking care not to block the lane.

) 47826, adorned with 'Scarborough Spa Express' branding, heads towards Harrogate with a tour from Scotland.
Photo by Phil Mason, June, 16:15, 55mm

Knaresborough Viaduct

Location Notes

Riverside views overlooking the viaduct across the River Nidd with the option to climb the cliff steps up towards Knaresbrough Castle for a view overlooking the viaduct.

1) Taken from the eastern bank of the Nidd, to the north of the viaduct. A pair of units head back to Leeds. *July, 17:15, 35mm*

Public Transport

Knaresborough Railway station is well served by Northern Rail trains from both York and Leeds.

Amenities

There are a few riverside cafes and bars as well as public toilets at the foot of the cliff. The town has a number of pubs, newsagents and cafes, but seems a little short of fast food outlets.

Accommodation

Knaresborough is a tourist resort and has a wide range of hotels, guest houses and B&Bs but will be busy during the tourist season.

Photographic Notes

From the northern side of the viaduct there is a view from the riverside looking up at the viaduct, with a couple of angle options along the 'Waterside'. You then follow 'Waterside' under the viaduct for more

2) From the western shore. A pair of 150s slow to stop. *July, 17:15, 35mm*

views of the viaduct from the southern side. Once again you can shoot from the waters edge looking up. Alternatively you can climb the steps up towards the castle and gain a view overlooking the viaduct itself. The area is busy with tourists and the steps themselves may not be suitable to set up tripods for video work but the castle ground has plenty of space. There is little extra noise other than a weir just round the river bend and the general noise produced by the public to interfere with video sound tracks. However, you are a fair distance away from the source.

Knaresborough Viaduct

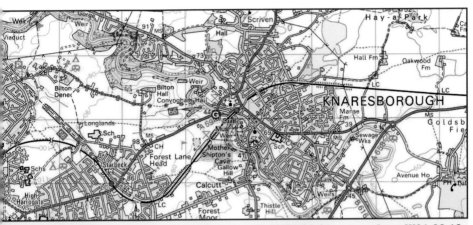

ostcode: HG5 8DP **Lat N54:00:31** **Long W01:28:19**

Road Directions

rom the A1(M), Junction 47: Head west along the A59 following the signs for Knaresborough. After just
ver 2 miles you will reach the town.

you continue through the town on the A59 you will eventually go down a hill with a large stone wall on
e right and a small green on the left. Just after this is the 'Worlds End' pub and the left turning onto
/aterside. On quiet days you may be able to park here. If you turn right there is a pay and display car
ark a hundred yards or so up the road but if you plan to visit during the summer months it would be worth
rriving well in advance as parking will be difficult to find.

) 70013 restarts a 'Scarborough Spa Express' from the station while heading for Leeds.
Photo by Phil Mason, August, 10:15, 50mm

The Stray

Location Notes
A footbridge across the line joining two sides of a large park in Harrogate.

1) Forming the tail end of a Harrogate Flower Special, 47802 heads south towards Leeds.
   Photo by Brian Russell, April, 12:30, 65mm

Public Transport
The location is about 10 minutes walk from Harrogate station which is well served by Northern Rail workings from Leeds and York.

Amenities
Just to the north of the park, on Station Parade, is a Waitrose supermarket. Further on is Harrogate town centre with the usual array of shops and fast food outlets.

Accommodation
Harrogate has a wide range of hotels and B&B, the closest being a Best Western on Tewit Well Road to the south.

2) Taken from the park.153359 heads south towards Leeds
   Photo by Brian Russell, February, 15:00, mm

Photographic Notes
The line is straight coming out of Harrogate station via the short tunnel. It is just possible to see southbound trains exiting the tunnel if you crouch, giving you plenty of notice of approaching workings. The bridge sides are low and would be suited to video work on a tripod. There is only the noise of people in the park to intrude on audio sound tracks.

The Stray

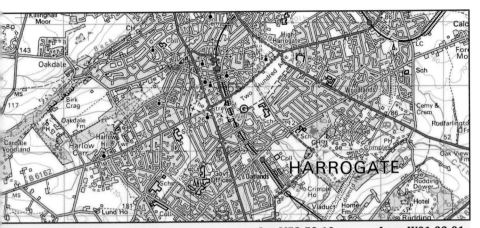

Postcode: HG2 8HX   **Lat N53:59:10**   **Long W01:32:01**

Road Directions

From the A1(M) Junction 47: Take the A59 west towards Harrogate. Although the A59 will take you to Harrogate it is best to avoid Knaresborough's narrow streets. So, when you reach a roundabout after about 2½ miles, take the A658 towards Bradford and then, after about 4 miles, take the A661 back towards Harrogate. Once in Harrogate you will drive through the parks. At the roundabout take the A6040 towards the Town Centre. At the junction with the traffic lights turn left on Stray Rein. At the bottom end of the park, by the houses on the right, is the path to the bridge.
You can park on the roadside in the park area.

3) After an unlikely start point at Sudbury in Essex, 47847 runs this charter's ECS to York Holgate via Leeds.
Photo by Brian Russell, September, 13:30, 85mm

Pannal, Buttersyke Bridge

Location Notes

A road over bridge to the south of the village of Burn Bridge.

1) 60076 pauses at the end of a possession during rail head replacement works on the line.
Photo by Brian Russell, September, 11:15, 70mm

Public Transport

The location is about a 10 minutes walk from Pannal station, via footpaths and roads, which is well served by Northern Rail workings from Leeds and York.

Amenities

There is 'The Black Swan' pub in Burn Bridge and 'The Harwood' pub opposite Pannal Station.

Accommodation

Just up the road from the bridge, in Burn Bridge, is the Willow Farm B&B.

Photographic Notes

The bridge sides are low, so a step ladder is not required. Both sides have a narrow

2) 66020 with auto ballasters at the foot crossing.
Photo by David Russel, September, 15:30, 45mm

grass verge and you are close to traffic passing as there is no pavement. Whistle boards for the foot crossing, to the north of the bridge, will alert you of southbound workings. The foot crossing also offers views in both directions.

Pannal, Butterskyke Bridge

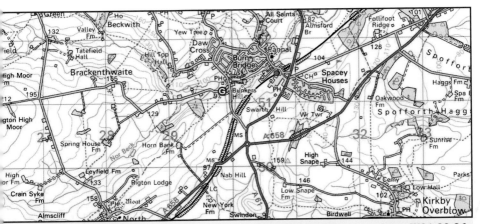

Postcode: HG3 1PF **Lat N53:57:08** **Long W01:32:36**

Road Directions

From the A1(M) Junction 47: Take the A59 west towards Harrogate. Then, after about 2½ miles, take the A658 towards Bradford. Follow this road for about 7 miles. At the roundabout where the A61 crosses the road turn right towards Harrogate. Shortly after the roundabout take the left turn signed 'Burn Bridge'. The bridge is a short distance up this road.

There is space to park 2 cars on the verge off road just to the south of the bridge, but it would be necessary to continue past the bridge and turn round to the other side of the road to park there safely. If you cannot park there then you will need to continue into Burn Bridge and walk back.

3) Heading south towards Leeds, 153363 accelerates away from a stop at Pannal station.
July, 16:30, 75mm

Rigton

Location Notes

A former farm track crossing, recently converted to a footpath crossing, opposite the A658.

1) Captured from the A658 side, 150269 heads west back to Leeds, providing the traction standard for the loop.
July, 16:00, 105mm

Public Transport

The location is about 15 minutes walk from Weeton station which is well served by Northern Rail workings from Leeds and York. Harrogate Coach Travel, Service X53, and Dales and District, Service 767, run from Harrogate Bus station to stops on the A658 near the location.

Amenities

There is nothing at the location, but there a few local shops in Huby.

Accommodation

There is nothing in the immediate area, the best option is to head back to York.

Photographic Notes

The line is reasonably straight past the crossing and the gates. Both sides of the line are flanked by trees but the southern side is broken up. The northern side is quite thick but this partially shields the location from the noise of passing traffic, making it suitable for videographers.

2) 150223 heads back to Knaresborough.
July, 16:00, 130mm

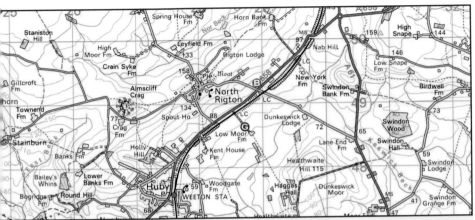

Postcode: LS17 0DZ   **Lat N53:56:06**   **Long W01:33:59**

Road Directions

From the A1(M) Junction 47: Take the A59 west towards Harrogate. Then, after about 2½ miles, take the A658 towards Bradford. Follow this road for about 7 miles. After the roundabout where the A61, to Pannal and Harewood, intersects the A658 continue straight across the roundabout. A sharp right takes you across the railway. Continue along the road, there is a brown tourist sign to the 'Square and Compass' just before the crossroads. The crossing is about ¼ mile over the crossroads.

You can park one car, off road, at the crossing on the verge. But if that is taken you will have to return to the crossroads, turn left and park on Hall Green Lane.

3) Just around the corner, 150223 accelerates away from Weeton station and approaches the crossing from the east.
July, 16:00, 300mm

Bramhope Tunnel, South

Location Notes

A footbridge across the line to the south of the 2 mile Bramhope tunnel. The bridge has a path, but the sides are often overgrown with tall weeds which will needs to be trampled to get to the sides.

1) An infrequent outing for a Pacer on a Leeds-bound shuttle. 142084 emerges from the tunnel.
July, 15:00, 65mm

Public Transport

Hosforth Railway station is about 30 minutes walk away, using footpaths to the west of the line. First Leeds, Service 96, runs frequently from Leeds City Bus Station (Stand 20) to a bus stop on Cockridge Lane.

Amenities

There is nothing in the immediate area so you should bring supplies with you.

Accommodation

The A660 has two larger hotels and in Leeds there is a range of hotels and guest houses.

Photographic Notes

As the location is a cutting, shadows can be a problem but in the later part of the morning the portal is lit. The signal clears when a southbound working is approaching, giving you some notice. The location is generally quiet, except for the aircraft at Leeds International Airport. This makes it a gamble for audio recordings.

2) 153363 disappears into the tunnel.
July, 15:15, 300mm

Bramhope Tunnel, South

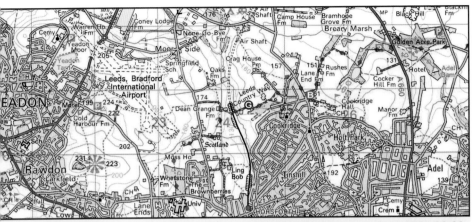

Postcode: LS16 7NG   **Lat N53:51:41**   **Long W01:38:02**

Road Directions

Get onto the A6120 from the either the M1, Junction 46 (via the A63 heading north), or from the A647 off the Bradford ring road. In Weetwood, take the A660 north towards Skipton (also signed Airport). Shortly after the roundabout there is a fork off the road towards Cookridge (Otley Old Road) take this. After about 2 miles you will see a zebra crossing with a turning to 'Ridgeside' on the right and just after the crossing a left turn onto Cookridge Drive, take this. Just as the road bears to the left turn right onto Craig Hill Avenue and then next left onto Smithy Lane. Smithy Lane leads to the location.

Although you can drive all the way down Smithy Lane, there are private residences at the end and it is only a bridleway. Park at the crossroads and walk down the Lane. After the last house the lane continues down a slightly narrower track. The bridge is at the bottom.

3) 155343 heads for Knaresborough with a northbound shuttle from Leeds.
July, 15:15, 140mm

Armley Junction

Location Notes

A tall footbridge affording views over the line to Skipton where the Harrogate loop rejoins the main line.

1) 153343 heads back around the circle towards Harrogate and, ultimately, Knaresborough.
July, 13:00, 35mm

Public Transport

The location is about a 20 minute walk from the Leeds main railway station. Alternatively First Bradford, Service 72, calls close to the location and operates very frequently from the Bus Station.

Amenities

The industrial area often has burger vans. Otherwise there is a Tesco Express ¾ mile up the Armley Road to the west.

Accommodation

You are about 20 minutes walk from the centre of Leeds which has a large number of hotels and guest houses.

Photographic Notes

The best shot from the bridge is of workings coming off the Harrogate loop, just before they go under the overhead wires. For this shot lens lengths of 100mm and greater are required. The two lines off the loop are bi-directional but the points should give clues as to which line the working is approaching on.
Shots of trains on the Skipton lines are possible but will require an artistic approach as you are almost directly above the westbound line. The side of the bridge is high so a step ladder would be an advantage. The bridge is opposite a busy main road and is also a reasonable distance from the lines so audio recordings are likely to be poor.

Armley Junction

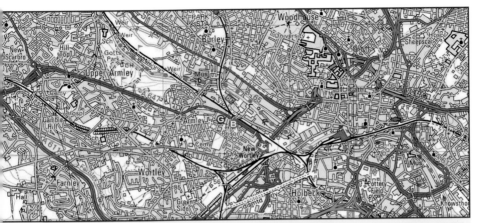

Postcode: LS12 2ER   **Lat N53:47:52**   **Long W01:34:27**

Road Directions

From the M621, Junction 2: Head north on the A643 towards Headingley Stadium. Follow the signs for the A58 and Station. Opposite the roundhouse (formerly the engine shed of the Leeds and Thirsk Railway) take the left turn onto Armley Road. Follow the road to the end and you will see the bridge on the left. Park on one of the side streets.

2) The return leg of an SRPS tour to Glenrothes leaves the loop and rejoins the main line.
   Photo by Mark Allatt, June, 17:00, 100mm

The Aire Valley and Branches

General Notes

The River Aire flows into the broad flood plain of the Aire Valley south of Skipton and then through the old industrial towns of Keighley, Bingley, Saltaire and Shipley, where the river meets Bradford Beck and then heads past Esholt, through Apperley Bridge and on to Leeds. The whole landscape is rolling hills and valleys. The main passenger lines are two track throughout, with only the Shipley to Esholt Junction section singled. There are 25kv overhead wires on all passenger routes, with the limit of electrification to the west of Skipton.

1) An unidentified 333 heads west through Cononley to Skipton.
July, 11:00, 80mm

Passenger Traffic

The lines are operated by Northern Rail, using Class 333 electric units between Skipton and Leeds, Bradford and Ilkley. Various Northern Rail Class 142, 153, 150 and 158 units work the non-electrified services from Leeds to destinations such as Morecambe and Carlisle.

Freight Traffic

There are steady flows of coal, stone and gypsum along the route from the Settle & Carlisle line. The quarry at Rylstone provides a couple of trains each day. These workings come off the Grassington branch and run round at Skipton before continuing east to Leeds and beyond.

2) 60059 heads south between Rylstone and Scale House.
Photo by Phil Mason, August, 16:45, 450mm

Occasional Traffic

Frequent specials from the Settle & Carlisle line use the route to reach destinations on the east coast and in the Midlands. There are also occasional loco moves from the Keighley & Worth Valley Railway connection at Keighley, which produce a random selection of types.

The New Measurement Train pays the occasional visit, and other test trains pass through. The autumn RHTT traffic has recently produced DRS traction.

3) 48151 heads west at Utley with a York to Carlisle charter.
Photo by Marcus Fudge, July, 10:30, 95mm

The Aire Valley and Branches

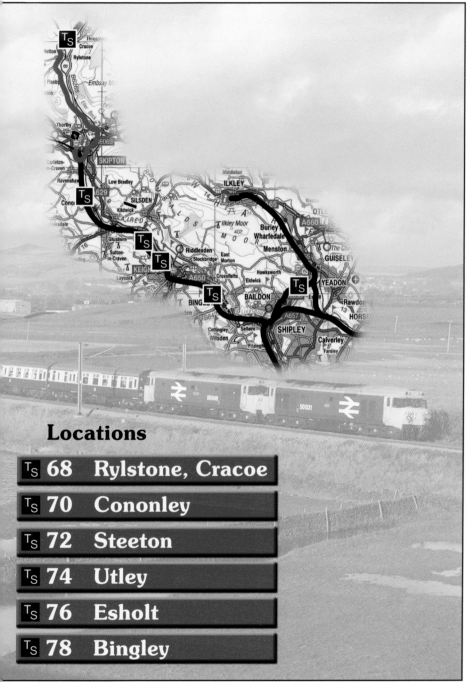

Locations

Rylstone, Cracoe

Location Notes

A few miles south of Rylstone quarry this is open farmland around the small village of Cracoe.

1) Of only minor interest to the resident goats 60059 ambles along the last mile with empties for Rylstone quarry.
Photo by Neil Harvey, July, 14:45, 40mm

Public Transport

Pride of the Dales, Service 72, operates an hourly service from Skipton Railway Station to the Devonshire Arms in Cracoe.

Amenities

Some of the local lay-bys have snack bars for the lorry drivers coming out of the quarry as well as the tourist traffic but these do not operate all year round. There is a cafe in the village and a small Farm Shop.

Accommodation

The Devonshire Arms offers bed and breakfast facilities in the village. Otherwise there are a number of B&Bs in Grassington to the north and Travel Inns around Skipton.

2) 60027 heads south with a loaded train for Hull.
Photo by Neil Harvey, September, 13:30, 40mm

Photographic Notes

The bridleway from the road goes under the railway and offers a number of angles on the line. You can also walk up the road to gain height over the line and a much wider view of the straight coming out of Rylstone quarry, which is a mile or so to the north. There are some electricity pylons and wires that can cause issues but careful positioning will avoid these.

The area is open farmland so, aside from wind, it is quiet and would suit videographers.

Rylstone, Cracoe

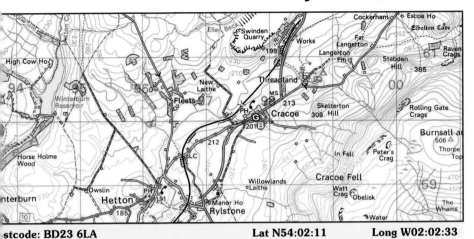

stcode: BD23 6LA   **Lat N54:02:11**   **Long W02:02:33**

oad Directions

om the northern end of the M65 follow the A6068, then A56, then A59 towards Skipton. At the undabout that is the junction with the A65 take the second exit - straight ahead on the A65. At the next undabout take the first exit - the B6265 towards Grassington. This road will lead you to Cracoe. On tering the village, just after the 40mph limit, the road dips down into the village and there is a turning on e left. There is room to park one or two cars in front of the house. To the side of the house is a path that ads to the location or you can go further along the road and look back from a higher vantage point.

60065 heads south with ex-National Power hoppers carrying material for the A1 widening scheme around Leeds.
Photo by Warren Armstrong, November, 11:30, fuj s3 @70mm

Cononley

Location Notes
A steep country road between Cononley and Glusburn.

1) 60045 heads for Rylstone. Please note, some farm sheds have been built and would now obscure the rear of the train
Photo by Neil Harvey, November, 14:00, 45mm

Public Transport
Cononley station is well served by Northern Trains services from Skipton and Leeds from where it is just over a mile walk.
Keighley and District, Service 78a, operates between Keighley Bus Station and Skipton. There is a stop at the bottom of the hill and opposite Cononley Station.

Amenities
There is a post office, village store and a few take-aways in Glusburn. In Cononley there is 'The Railway Pub' and 'New Inn', post office and village stores.

Accommodation
There is a bed and breakfast 'Cononley Hall' in the village.

Photographic Notes
The location is more of a 'train in the landscape' style shot than an 'close up ¾ view' but it will suit a wide variety of lens lengths. The road has small grass verges to stand on. You are looking over dry stone walls.
The open nature makes it very suitable for videographers. But traffic on the road, though not frequent, will be passing close behind you so be wary.

2) A 333 heads east towards Bradford.
July, 11:15, 65mm

Cononley

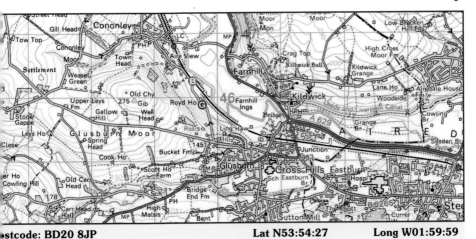

stcode: BD20 8JP   **Lat N53:54:27**   **Long W01:59:59**

oad Directions

om the end of the M65 continue along the A6068 for about 8 miles into Glusburn. Turn left, between two
uses, onto Green Lane. Follow this road to the end, turn right and then immediately left onto Cononley
ad. The location is on this road.
e road itself is not suitable for parking due to its width. There are some grass verges at the bottom of the
l where you could park but it would be better to park in Glusburn and walk down the hill to the location.

50031 and 50039 pass the flooded fields of Cononley, at the bottom of the hill, with a charter from Cardiff to Leeds.
Photo by Neil Harvey, December, 12:00, 45mm

Steeton

Location Notes
A scenic roadside, or up close field edge, view of the line.

1) A Northern Trains 333 pulls away from Steeton and Silsden station and heads east back to Leeds.
Photo by Peter Kellet, October, 18:30, 135mm

Public Transport
Steeton and Silsden station is served by Northern Trains services from Skipton and Leeds from where it would be about 10 minutes walk to the locations.
Keighley and District, Service 78a, operates between Keighley Bus Station and Skipton. There are a number of stops on Keighley Road for the location.

Amenities
There are the Goats Head Pub and a newsagents in Steeton.

2) 66199 heads a rake of empty gypsum boxes to Milford.
Photo by Mark Bearton, July, 15:00, 45mm

Accommodation
There is the Steeton Hall Hotel for luxury accommodation, but for more cost effective options you would be best heading back towards Keighley.

Photographic Notes
The roadside offers a wide view of workings, but is best suited to the later part of the morning for southbound, or from mid-afternoon for northbound workings. The proximity to the busy road would make this position unsuitable for audio recordings.
If you walk down the field edges you can get a closer shot of the line away from the noise of the passing road traffic. Alternatively you can walk down the footpath from the station for earlier morning views of Keighley bound workings.

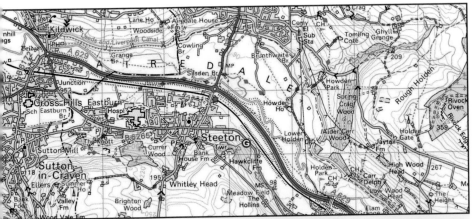

Postcode: BD20 6QR **Lat N53:53:44** **Long W01:56:20**

Road Directions

Take the A629 from either the end of the M65 (via the A6068) or the Bradford ring road until you reach the turning for Steeton. Follow the A6034 into Steeton, signed for the 'Airedale General Hospital'. Pass over the railway, continue to the traffic lights and turn left. This road leads to the location. It would, however, be better to park in Steeton village and walk to the location as there is no roadside parking available.

333013 heads towards Keighley. Taken from the footpath on the A629 side of the line.
Photo by Adam Parkinson, May, 15:45, 90mm

Utley

Location Notes

A foot crossing on a path adjoining the Utley area of Keighley town with fields and the river to the north.

1) 333015 heads away from the crossing and on to Skipton. Taken from the top of the style steps.
July, 12:15, 105mm

Public Transport

Keighley and District, Service 78a, operates between Keighley Bus Station and Skipton. If you alight near the Keighley Rugby club you can walk down to the line from the road, using paths around the pitches.

Amenities

There is the Roebuck Pub and Chinese take-away on the Skipton Road. Otherwise there are a couple of fast food outlets and a petrol station near the A629 roundabout.

Accommodation

There is the Dalesgate Hotel on Skipton Road. Otherwise Keighley has a number of options.

Photographic Notes

The crossing has a stile which can give you a height advantage from the lineside, while keeping a safe distance back. These steps are available on both sides of the line.

2) 333015 heads to Skipton with a local service from Leeds.
July, 12:15, 130mm

The fields only offer views from the northern side of the line so can be backlit on bright days. Traffic noise, from the A629 may be a problem for audio recordings.

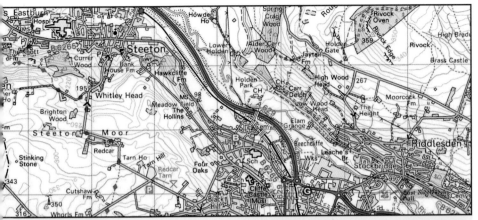

Postcode: BD21 3NJ   **Lat N53:53:08**   **Long W01:55:16**

Road Directions

Take the A629 from either the end of the M65 (via the A6068) or the Bradford ring road until you reach Keighley. If you are approaching from the west you will pass the location on your right, but you need to be on the westbound carriageway to park. From the A629 roundabout, after McDonalds, in Keighley continue up the A629 and you will soon pass under a road bridge. A short distance after this there is a signed lay-by where you should park.

From here use the stile and cross the field towards the railway to reach the location.

3) 5690 heads the first of four Keighley & Worth Valley Railway shuttles to Settle Junction.
  Photo by Marcus Fudge, June, 09:45, 55mm

Esholt

Location Notes

A picturesque viaduct on the Shipley to Ilkley branch line.

1) An unidentified 333 heads east toward Ilkley with a working from Bradford. Taken from the post office corner.
August, 09:45, 120mm

Public Transport

TLC Travel Limited, Service 653, operates between Bradford Interchange and Leeds Airport and passes Shipley Station. The stop at Hollins Hill, Station Road, is a few minutes from the location.
The location is about 1½ miles walk from Baildon station.

Amenities

In the village there is a small post office and 'The Woolpack' pub. This is the pub used in the Emmerdale television series until 1989. However, it was undergoing refurbishment at the time of the location visit.

Accommodation

There is a Marriott Hotel on Hollins Hill.

Photographic Notes

The viaduct has a hill, to the north west, that offers views from above the height of the train as well as roadside, from all directions, views looking up at the viaduct. The area is quiet apart from the odd passing car so is well suited for videographers.

2) A rare loco appearance on the viaduct by 66546.
Photo by Andrew Wade, October, 09:45, 50mm

Esholt

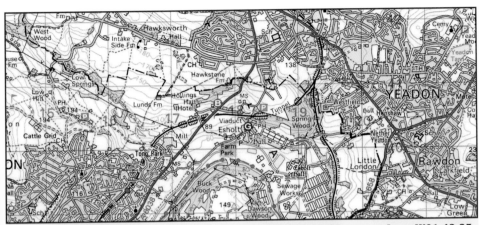

Postcode: BD17 7RB   **Lat N53:51:38**   **Long W01:43:35**

Road Directions

Take the A65 north from Leeds for about 8 miles to Guisley. At the larger roundabout after the 'Yorkshire Rose' pub turn left just after the KFC Drive-Thru, following the A6038 signs to Hawksworth. About a mile down the road is a turning on the left, there is a phone box on the corner, 'Old Hollings Hill' follow this road and at the junction at the end the viaduct is in front of you.

Park in the village and walk back towards the viaduct.

3) A stroll after visiting the pub reveals 333001 heading towards Bradford. .
Photo by Mark Bearton, August, 14:30, 80mm

Treaclecock Bridge, Bingley

Location Notes
A new footbridge, constructed in 2004, taking a footpath over the Bingley relief road and rail lines. It replaces a former tunnel under the rerouted Liverpool and Leeds Canal.

1) 333012 heads north with a Northern working for Skipton after calling at Bingley station in the background.
Photo by Phi Mason, November, 15:45, 65mm

Public Transport
The location is a 5-10 minute walk from Bingley station which is well served by Northern Trains.

Amenities
There are cafes, pubs and a post office on the High Street. There is also a petrol station next to the location.

Accommodation
Bingley has a range of hotels and B&Bs to suit all pockets.

Photographic Notes
The footbridge crosses over the line and offers tight head-on views from both sides in both directions. Given the proximity to the A650, road noise will be a serious issue for audio recordings. There is an alternative side-on shot from the other side of the canal looking back down the Three Locks to the

2) 37408 passes the Three Locks with a York to Carlisle working.
Photo by Neil Harvey, August, 10:00, 52mm

line. This is best suited to early mornings when the sun is in the east.
The bridge often smells as though there is a fire nearby. Don't worry, it's just training at the Fire Station!

Treaclecock Bridge, Bingley

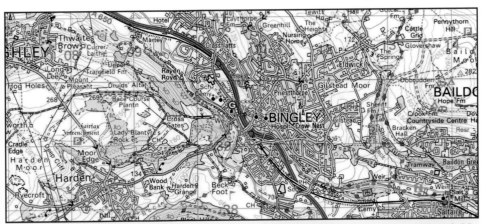

Postcode: BD16 2RD   **Lat N53:51:05**   **Long W01:50:22**

Road Directions

Leave the A650 in Bingley following signs for the station. When the station sign diverts off to the right by the Co-op car park continue straight on to the traffic lights staying in the right hand lane so you can turn right. Take this road all the way though the town centre. When you see the fire station on your right park up on the roadside and the footbridge is on the right.

3) 50031 and 50039 hammer past the A650 traffic with a charter from Cardiff to Leeds.
Photo by Phil Mason, December, 12:15, 75mm

Calder Valley Line

General Notes

The line follows the route of the Rochdale Canal from Manchester to Sowerby Bridge, until the canal joins with the River Ryburn to become the Calder and Hebble Navigation.

The line, which is double track throughout, has some steep grades and tunnels through the valleys. At Hall Royd Junction, just east of Todmorden, the Copy Pit line joins from Preston in the west. A loop via Oldham used to join the line at Rochdale, but this is currently under conversion to light rail use.

1) 153347 slows for the Castleton stop on a Leeds working
Photo by Adam Parkinson, September, 11:25, 120mm

Passenger Traffic

Northern Trains operates the passenger services with Classes 144, 150, 153 and 158. They run from Manchester Victoria to Huddersfield, Leeds and Knottingley.

Freight Traffic

Little freight traffic uses the route as heavy trains are more suited to the flatter Trans Pennine route to the east. Lighter freight movements, such as units for refurbishment, often travel this way to save paths on the busier Trans Pennine. Obviously, these run on an 'as required' basis.

2) 66561 heads south at Eastwood with diverted coal empties.
Photo by Adam Parkinson, September, 10:15, 130mm

Occasional Traffic

The line is often used for locomotive movements to and from the East Lancashire Railway at Bury, which has a connection to the main line from the Castleton triangle. Tours also start from the East Lancashire Railway to destinations around the country. The 'Cotton Mills Express' regularly uses the route in the summer. If there is a problem on the Trans Pennine route, traffic will be diverted this way.

MPV units based at Wigan usually operate the autumn RHTT traffic. They also cover some of the smaller branch lines.

3) 67006 on the tail of the 'Northen Belle' at Dobroyd.
Photo by Adam Parkinson, July, 08:15, 75mm

Calder Valley Line

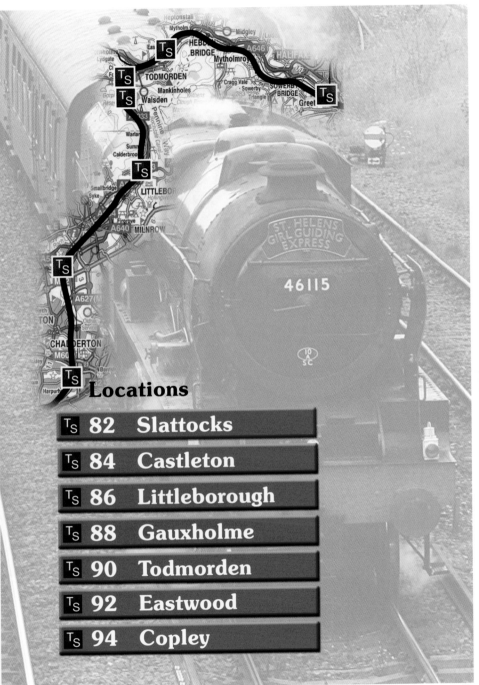

Locations

Slattocks

Location Notes

A road bridge on a busy route from the M62 into Middleton, situated to the north of Manchester.

1)150133 heads north, away from the camera, with a local working from Manchester Victoria to Rochdale.
July, 18:45, 35mm

Public Transport

First, Service 17, runs from Rochdale into Manchester. The service also passes Castleton station and stops either side of the bridge.

Amenities

There is the 'Ship Inn' by the roundabout, opposite the Rochdale Canal and a petrol station just up the Rochdale Road.

Accommodation

There is the 'Three Gates' B&B just to the east tucked away, between the distribution centre and the A627M, on Stakehill Lane.

Photographic Notes

The bridge and approaches offer head-on views from the west and head-on and side views from the east. There are trees lining the roadside restricting the angles you can take. However, there are angles allowing for 3 or 4 coaches of a train to be shot with the rest tailing off behind

2) 155343 heads north with a local Rochdale working.
July, 18:30, 60mm

the trees. Both sides of the bridge parapets are high and a step ladder would be an advantage.

The shot of northbound workings is difficult as it has to be taken from a side of the bridge with a very small pavement, about a foot wide.

Due to noise from the road the location is unsuitable for video recordings.

Slattocks

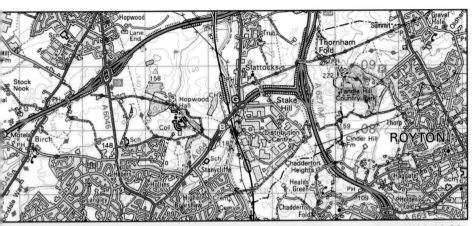

ostcode: M24 2RN   **Lat N53:34:14**   **Long W02:10:39**

oad Directions

rom the M62, Junction 20: Take the A627(M) south towards Oldham and then take the A664 towards iddleton and Castleton. At the first roundabout take the fourth exit (right turn) onto the A664 towards astleton. Find somewhere to park on this road and then walk back to the roundabout, turn right and walk p to the bridge.

3) Still accelerating away from Castleton junction 37405 and 422 head south with Metrolink ballast empties
Photo by Jim Murphy, April, 11:00, 115mm

Castleton

Location Notes

A road bridge and side road on the approaches to the former yard at Castleton.

1) 158757 clatters across the pointwork into the once-great yard at Castleton while heading north to Leeds.
July, 19:00, 120mm

Public Transport

The bridge is just above Castleton station which is well served by Northern trains from Manchester, Rochdale to Leeds and Huddersfield.

Amenities

The bridge is on Castleton High Street, which has a wide range of shops, takeaways and pubs.

Accommodation

There is nothing in the immediate area, but there is a Travel Inn at J22 of the M62.

Photographic Notes

The bridge sides are reasonably high so a step ladder may be an advantage.

2) After failing earlier 46115 is 'attended to' in Castleton Yard.
Photo by Adam Parkinson, July, 17:15, 170mm

Heywood Road, which runs parallel to the line offers a range of heights over the line from bridge height to track level. There is the usual palisade fence along the side of the road combined with some large bushes so a step ladder is essential. From the end of the road you can look through the gates.

Traffic noise and the parapet height would make videoing difficult from the bridge and the fences would also hinder videos, making this location unsuitable for videographers.

Castleton

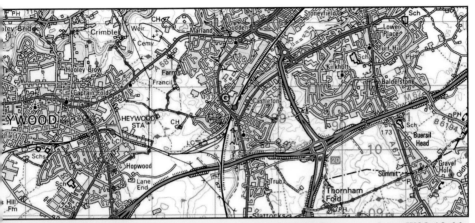

ostcode: OL11 3EE   **Lat N53:35:31**   **Long W02:10:44**

Road Directions

From the M62, Junction 20: Take the A627(M) north towards Rochdale. Keep in the left hand lane for Rochdale and filter left at the roundabout. Continue along this road until the next roundabout where once again you need to keep left and filter left at the traffic lights. After passing the large Tesco on your left you will come to another set of traffic lights, this used to be a roundabout and is marked on the map as such, but it is now a junction. Go straight on in the A664 lane, passing the blue building on your left and go up the hill. Continue along this road for about a mile and you will reach Castleton Station. There is a turning on the right signed to Holyrood Nursery which is Heywood Road. Turn down here and park.

3) 67002 heads north towards Leeds while moving 508120 from Birkenhead to Doncaster for refurbishment.
Photo by Adam Parkinson, June, 18:15, 225mm

Gale, Littleborough

Location Notes

A footbridge with houses to the west and small factories, along Weighver's Way, to the east.

1) 144015 coasts south towards Littleborough, and then Manchester Victoria, after the long slog up to Summit Tunnel.
July, 17:15, 85mm

Public Transport

First Calderdale and Huddersfield, Service 590, operates from Rochdale Bus Station and calls at stops on the main road opposite Reddyshore Brow.
The location is about 2½ miles walk from Littleborough Station which is served by trains from Manchester and Leeds.

Amenities

There is nothing in the immediate area but Littleborough has a generous range of shops in the town centre.

Accommodation

There is nothing locally but there are a few hotels in Littleborough and a few B&Bs around Hollingworth Lake to the south.

2) 150146 tails a northbound Northern service to Leeds.
July, 16:25, 300mm

Photographic Notes

The bridge offers views in both directions and is one of the last bridges before the 1½ mile long Summit tunnel. Northbound workings will be climbing up towards the summit at this point. The bridge parapets are reasonably high and a step ladder. The location is reasonably quiet and would be well suited to videographers with tall tripods. There is a signal just before the bridge's northern side which would hinder wide angle shots, requiring 70mm+ lenses to shoot past.

Gale, Littleborough

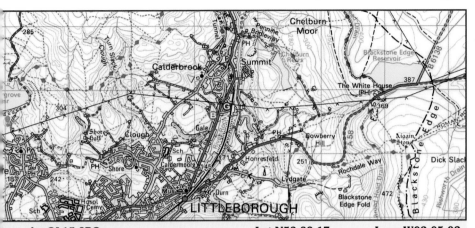

Postcode: OL15 9PQ   Lat N53:39:17   Long W02:05:02

Road Directions

From the M62, Junction 21: Take the A640 north towards Milnrow. In Milnrow the road splits into two lanes. Keep in the right hand lane and turn into the B6225. Then follow the sign left and take the B6225 to Littleborough. Shortly after passing over the canal in Littleborough turn left under the railway viaduct on the A58 towards Rochdale and then second left, by the church, onto the A6033 towards Todmorden. Follow this road for about a mile until you reach a right turn onto 'Reddyshore Brow'. Follow this road down and over a tiny river bridge and park.

In Shottwood Fold, to the left, there is a footpath between the houses that leads, via a gate, to the bridge.

144003 does the donkey work on the climb to Summit Tunnel with a Northern working to Leeds.
July, 16:15, 130mm

Gauxholme Viaduct

Location Notes

A viaduct carrying the line over Walsden, Todmorden and the Rochdale Canal.

1) #1 Looking down from Pexwood Road. 153345 heads away from the camera towards Manchester.
   Photo by Mark Bearton, May, 14:30, 80mm

Public Transport

The location is mid way between Todmorden Station to the north and Walsden Station to the south. Both are served by trains from Manchester Victoria and Leeds, although not all trains stop at Walsden. First Calderdale and Huddersfield, Service 589, operates hourly between Burnley and Rochdale Bus stations and passes the location.

Amenities

There are a few pubs on the road to Todmorden and a Morrisons Store further up.

Accommodation

There are several B&Bs and hotels in Todmorden close to the railway station.

Photographic Notes

The viaduct and bridge pass over towns and the vantage points on either side are some distance apart so it is best to plan for the direction of the working you are shooting. Both shots are from the

2) #2 37423 pushes Caroline north Todmorden bound.
   Photo by Mike Taylor, September, 16:00, 45mm

west of the line so would suit afternoon and evening shots. Southbound workings will be climbing up the hill towards Summit Tunnel which is a few miles to the south.

From the northern vantage point the bridge sides will obscure a shot in the northbound direction, unless shot outside the summer when the line side vegetation has died down.

For videographers there is only the distant noise of the town but because of the distance you are unlikely to hear anything other than general noise.

Gauxholme Viaduct

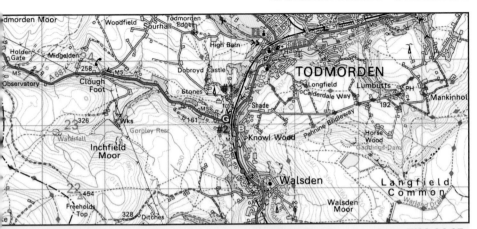

Postcode: OL14 7PW   **Lat N53:42:15**   **Long W02:06:27**

Road Directions

From the M62, Junction 24: Take the A629 north towards Hailfax and then take the A6026 towards Sowerby Bridge at the junction. Continue along the road and at the next set of lights turn left down into Sowerby Bridge. Following the signs to Burnley take the A646 north out of Sowerby Bridge and follow the road until you reach Todmorden. At the roundabout in front of the church in Todmorden turn left and follow the A6033 towards Bacup.

Soon you will reach the viaduct and see the A681 turn to Bacup which will take you under the viaduct. Once under the viaduct you can turn right to go up Pexwood Road to reach vantage point #1. There is room to park towards the top of the hill.

For vantage point #2 park after the viaduct and continue on foot up the road. On the left next to a builders yard is the bridleway, left out of Naze Road that will lead you up the hill to the other location.

#2) #2 185113 takes a diverted Trans Pennine service south towards Manchester.
Photo by Paul Bigland, September, 16:00, 85mm

Dobroyd Road, Todmorden

Location Notes

A small foot crossing to the south of the railway station. The lane is an access back road connecting Todmorden Village with the Dobroyd Castle estate.

1) 153332 heads south towards Manchester Victoria after departing from Todmorden station.
Photo by Adam Parkinson, May, 09:15, 90mm

Public Transport

Todmorden has a regular rail service, operated by Northern Rail, from Manchester and Leeds

Amenities

On the other side of the main road is a Morrisons supermarket. Further down the road is a Chinese takeaway and there are more options further down the road.

Accommodation

Todmorden has a range of B&Bs and hotels. The tourist information office is directly across the road from the Rail Station.

Photographic Notes

The crossing is on a quiet footpath. The path climbs up to the crossing from the eastern side and then continues to climb on the other. It offers a range of heights over southbound subjects. The view of northbound workings is hindered by the tree line.

There is room to set up video tripods and aside from the rustling of the trees there is very little to interfere with audio sound tracks.

2) 158753 heads south towards a snowy Manchester.
Photo by Adam Parkinson, December, 12:15, 90mm

Dobroyd Road, Todmorden

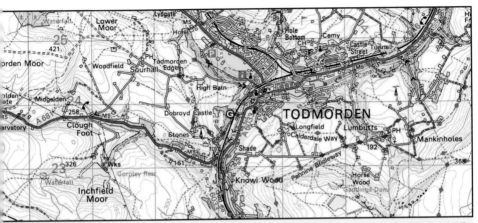

Postcode: OL14 7LU   **Lat N53:42:38**   **Long W02:06:13**

Road Directions

From the M62, Junction 24: Take the A629 north towards Hailfax and then take the A6026 towards Sowerby Bridge at the junction. Continue along the road and at the next set of lights turn left down into Sowerby Bridge. Following the signs to Burnley take the A646 north out of Sowerby Bridge and follow the road until you reach Todmorden. At the roundabout in front of the church in Todmorden turn left and follow the A6033 towards Bacup. Park in Morrisons car park, unless you plan to stay for more than 2 hours. Situated between the main car park entrance and the deliveries entrance, but on the opposite side of the road is Dobroyd Road. Walk up here to access the foot crossing.

3) Running the Northern Belle rather than the Royals 67005 heads north towards Todmorden.
Photo by Adam Parkinson, July, 08:15, 60mm

Eastwood

Location Notes
An open lattice footbridge over the line where recent tree clearance has taken place, opening up the shot.

1) 47815 top & tails with 47843 on a Runcorn to Edinburgh charter.
Photo by Ross Byers, June, 08:30, 55mm

Public Transport
First Calderdale and Huddersfield, Service 594, runs between Halifax and Rochdale Bus Stations, passing Hebden Bridge and Todmorden Stations and calling at Jumble Hole Road.

Amenities
There is nothing on the main road, Hebden Bridge is about a mile to the north with a range of shops.

Accommodation
There is the Badger Fields B&B in Blackshaw Head or a range of places in Hebden Bridge

Photographic Notes
The line runs north east to south west so suits northbound workings in the early morning and southbound workings after that until mid-afternoon. The bridge is of an open lattice design so a step ladder is not required. It is a popular location so it can be busy when specials are due.
There are also wider options from the lanes to the east, or an afternoon angle from the path up from Jumble Hole Lane.
The road is far enough away to not be a major problem for audio sound tracks and the bridge is quite wide so should be suitable for videographers.

2) 45407 heads south over Jumble Hole Bridge.
Photo by Robert Green, November, 13:15, 75mm

3) With the bridge behind it, 158753 heads south.
Photo by Mark Bearton, April, 11:45, 70mm

Eastwood

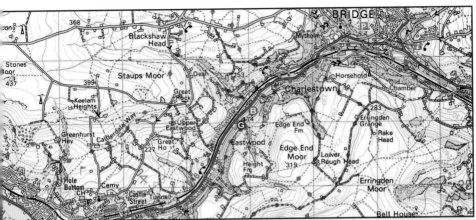

Postcode: OL14 6EQ   **Lat N53:43:54**   **Long W02:02:60**

Road Directions

From the M65, Junction 8: Take the A56 south and then turn left on the A679 towards Accrington. Just after the road runs parallel to the canal there is a set of traffic lights. Get in the right hand lane and follow the A646 to the location.

From the M62, Junction 24: Take the A629 north until you reach the junction with the A646, in Siddal, towards Burnley.

There is a sewage works to the north of the location, opposite is a side road, Jumble Hole Road, where you can park and walk to the location - either up Jumble Hole Road and left or back down the main road.

4) 60100 in winter sun while hauling an additional continuous welded rail train from Scunthorpe to Crewe.
Photo by Nigel Cockburn, February, 11:45, 70mm

Copley, Milner Royd Junction

Location Notes

An open view over the Calderdale Valley. From here you can see the line diverging to Bradford Interchange at Milner Royd Junction, behind the line to Leeds via Mirfield.

1) A Northern Rail 158 cruises across Copley viaduct, away from the camera, towards Halifax.
Photo by Paul Bigland, October, 12:45, 250mm

Public Transport

The Huddersfield Coach Company, Services 557 and 559, operate from Halifax Bus Station to Norland, Clough Road. This is then a short downhill walk to the location.

Amenities

There is nothing in the immediate area, but Sowerby Bridge has a wide range of shops.

Accommodation

Halifax and Sowerby Bridge are a short drive away with a range of Hotels and B&Bs

Photographic Notes

Another "train in the landscape" shot. The foreground line, from Mirfield, is little used and the lineside trees provide a major obstruction during the summer months. During the rest of the year the shot opens up. The shot requires telephoto lenses to give some detail, with a

2) 150266 comes off the viaduct on its way to Halifax.
Photo by Michael McNicholas, April, 10:40, 200mm

minimum length of 80mm recommended. Videographers may prefer the likes of steam specials here as the added height should give the smoke some extra perspective. You are however half a mile away from your subject so you will not hear much. There is no shot looking west as this is masked by the hillside. There are alternative shots of the viaduct from Copley Lane, just off the A6026.

Copley, Milner Royd Junction

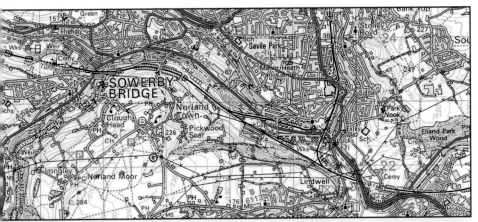

Postcode: HX6 3QZ   **Lat N53:42:08**   **Long W01:52:49**

Road Directions

From the M62, Junction 24: Take the A629 towards Hailfax, turning left at the traffic lights onto the A6026 towards Sowerby Bridge. Continue along the road and at the next set of lights turn left down into Sowerby Bridge. Following the road you will reach Sowerby Bridge. Upon entering the village and passing the 30mph signs there is a turning on the left that takes you down to a narrow bridge. Cross the bridge and continue straight along the road up the tree lined lane. You will pass over the railway line and then climb up to a T junction where you should turn left. Continue up this steep road until you reach a 'no through road sign'. This is the location. There is a small area to park just down the no through road.

3) 67002 with the Cleethorpes to Blackpool section of the 'Coast to Coast' charter from Euston.
Photo by Neil Harvey, March, 15:40, 95mm

Trans Pennine Route

General Notes

From From the conurbation of Greater Manchester the landscape soon opens up into the open hills and mountains of the Pennines, which the line bisects between Stalybridge and Huddersfield. The line follows the route of the Huddersfield Canal, and features the three mile Standedge tunnel. Once the line breaks out of Standedge at Marsden, there is a short section of open countryside which soon translates into another urban sprawl running almost continuously from Huddersfield to Leeds.

1) 185125 rounds the curve at Marsden with a Leeds train.
Photo by Mark Allatt, March, 13:45, 120mm

Passenger Traffic

Northern Trains operates local services between Manchester Victoria and Sheffield to Huddersfield and Leeds, worked by Class 150s, 144s and 156s. TransPennine Express operates Class 185 units and the occasional Class 170 from Manchester, Sheffield and Liverpool to Middlesbrough, Newcastle and Scarborough.

Freight Traffic

There are a few freight flows along the Manchester to Thornhill (Healey Mills) section of the route. The primary traffic is the 'binliner' from Northenden in South Manchester to Roxby on Humberside. There are odd cement flows from Leeds to Tunstead and wagons heading for repair. Mirfield also receives traffic from the Copy Pit line and Rochdale routes heading east.

2) 60020 heads through Paddock Cutting with the Roxby binliner.
Photo by Nigel Cockburn, August, 12:00, 40mm

Occasional Traffic

The Pennine section is a popular route for charters from Manchester to Leeds but, because of pathing constraints on the Dewsbury section, they often reach Leeds via Normanton. The 'Cotton Mills Express' is a regular visitor in the summer months. The New Measurement Train and other Serco test trains also turn up on test duties, as well as in transit. Autumn RHTT trains are worked by traction from either DB Schenker or DRS.

3) 56078 exits Standedge Tunnel with a charter to York.
Photo by Albert Dawson, March, 15:00, 60mm

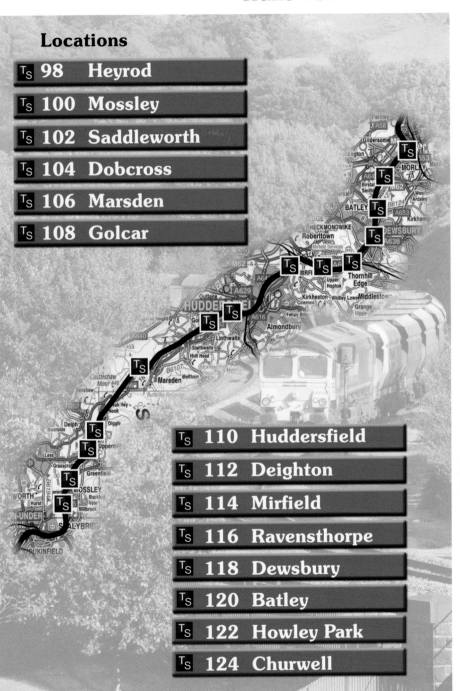

Locations

ᵀS	98	Heyrod
ᵀS	100	Mossley
ᵀS	102	Saddleworth
ᵀS	104	Dobcross
ᵀS	106	Marsden
ᵀS	108	Golcar

ᵀS	110	Huddersfield
ᵀS	112	Deighton
ᵀS	114	Mirfield
ᵀS	116	Ravensthorpe
ᵀS	118	Dewsbury
ᵀS	120	Batley
ᵀS	122	Howley Park
ᵀS	124	Churwell

Black Rock, Heyrod

Location Notes

A footbridge over the line about 1 mile south of Mossley Station and a short distance from the site of the former Black Rock sidings and signal box.

1) 37423 gives saloon Caroline a shove, away from the camera, while heading south towards Manchester.
Photo by Chris Throp, June, 14:45, 75mm

Public Transport

Mossley Station is about a mile to the north and is served by hourly trains from Manchester Victoria and Huddersfield. From the station it is about a 20 minute walk to the bridge.
Greater Manchester PTE, Services 353 and 354, run from Stalybridge Station to 'Wakefield Road, Heyrod which is opposite the location.

Amenities

There is a village store in Heyrod Village about ½ mile south of the bridge.

Accommodation

The 'Flushing Meadow' Guest House is in Heyrod Village on the western side of the A635 just by the 'Welcome to Heyrod' village sign.

Photographic Notes

The line runs roughly north to south under the bridge but the line itself is on an 'S' bend through the location. This means there is little notice of approaching workings.
There are options for an early morning shot of Huddersfield bound workings from the eastern side of the bridge. Once the sun has come round, the Manchester, southbound, shot is on until mid-afternoon when the sun will go behind the hills.
The bridge has an open lattice design and a step ladder will not be required. It is also reasonably wide and although the A635 will produce traffic noise the sound of passing workings should drown this out.

Black Rock, Heyrod

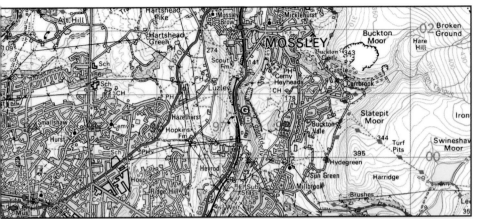

Postcode: OL5 9QB   **Lat N53:30:09**   **Long W02:02:34**

Road Directions

From the M60, Junction 23: Take the A6140 or A635 exit towards Ashton-under-Lyme and follow the A635 for about 3 miles, watching for the speed cameras at the beginning of Heyrod Village.
Eventually the railway will appear on your right and you will come to a narrow bridge, protected by traffic lights that will take you under the railway. Shortly after crossing under the line you will see the footbridge up on your left. Park in one of the side streets.

2) 60082 heads south towards Manchester with the empty binliner.
Photo by Bevan Price, March, 15:00, 55mm

Mossley

Location Notes

A lattice footbridge over the line on a sharp curve about ¼ mile north of Mossley Station.

1) Taking out the Greater Manchester trash. 66527 heads north to Roxby.
Photo by Neil Harvey, March, 11:15, 75mm

Public Transport

Mossley station is about ¼ mile to the south and is served by hourly trains from Manchester Victoria and Huddersfield. From the station it is about a 10 minute walk to the bridge. Greater Manchester PTE, Services 353 and 354, run from Stalybridge Station to either Stockport Road, to the east opposite the 'Church Inn' Pub, or Manchester Road to the west depending on the service. From either, walk down Roughtown Road to reach the bridge.

Amenities

On the Stockport Road, up the hill, there is the 'Church Inn' and 'The Billy Goat' Pub, The 'Woodend Tavern' is on Manchester Road. There are also newsagents and cafes in Mossley opposite the station.

Accommodation

There is the 'Hartshead Hotel' in Hartshead Green which offers Bed and Breakfast.

Photographic Notes

The line rounds a sharp curve, southbound that is well lit throughout the later part of the morning. In the early morning northbound shots are favourably lit. From about mid afternoon the sun goes behind the hills and throws the whole location into shadow.

2) 5690 climbs to Standedge summit.
Photo by Robert Green, September, 11:15, 95mm

The area is away from main roads so is reasonably quiet and the wide bridge is suitable for videographers, although the nature of the curve means you get very little warning of approaching workings.

Mossley

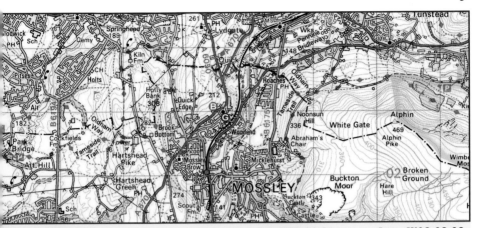

Postcode: OL5 0SH   **Lat N53:31:21**   **Long W02:02:09**

Road Directions

From the M60, Junction 23: Take the A6140 or A635 exit towards Ashton-under-Lyme and follow the A635 or 5 miles, watching for the speed cameras at the beginning of Heyrod Village and passing Mossley Station on the left. After passing the 'Woodend Tavern' on your right you will notice the houses on the left topping and trees starting. The left turn into Roughtown Road, to the location, is here but the turn is about 00 degrees so it is probably best to use the builders yard to do a U-turn and approach the road from the ther direction. Once up the typically narrow and steep Yorkshire hill you will see the bridge on the right nd space for one or two cars on the left. If these are full then you can park back on the Manchester Road.

3) With the slightly less-whiffy empty 'bins', 66546 rounds the bend on the downhill back to Northenden.
Photo by Neil Harvey, March, 13:15, 30mm

Saddleworth Viaduct

Location Notes

A high vantage point over the viaduct with views of the rolling hills in the background. Be aware that the cliff is not fenced in any way but you can stand a good 20 feet back from the cliff face and get the same shot. Although a completely safe location for sensible adults it is certainly not recommended for unsupervised children or vertigo sufferers!

1) #2 From the northern vantage point, 66124 heads north with the evening Stalybridge to Immingham tanks.
Photo by Neil Harvey, July, 19:30, 70mm

Public Transport

Greater Manchester PTE, Services 353 and 354, run from Stalybridge Station to stops on the High Street in Uppermill. From there is it a steep walk up the hills to the locations.

Amenities

Uppermill High Street has a number of small stores, take-aways and cafes.

Accommodation

Uppermill is rife with tourist facilities and has hotels and guest houses to suit all pockets.

2) 170304 Manchester-bound. Taken from the footpath.
Photo by John Rinder, March, 10:45, 35mm

Photographic Notes

Very much an afternoon shot as there are no angles from the east of the line. The standard vantage point #1 is best suited to afternoon or early evening shots when the sun has come round to the western side of the line. There is also an option from the footpath visible from the cliff top, but it is a long walk round. In the evening the fields between Sandy Lane and Sugar Lane, #1, offer another view.

All locations are free from noise and would be well suited to video, although you can be some distance from the subject.

3) Below #1, 66607 heads south with coal empties.
Photo by John Rinder, March, 10:45, 35mm

Saddleworth Viaduct

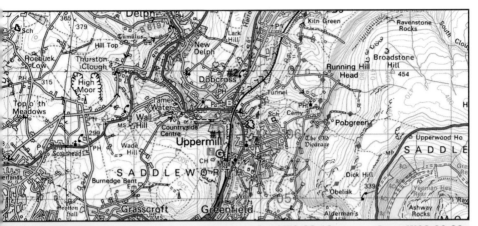

Postcode: OL3 6LT   **Lat N53:33:12**   **Long W02:00:29**

Road Directions

From the M62, Junction 22: Head south along the A672 towards Saddleworth.

From the M60, Junction 22: Head to Oldham on the A62, Saddleworth is signed as a Tourist Attraction. In Delph you will see a larger brown tourist sign for Saddleworth, proceed into the village and turn right onto the A6052 towards Dobcross and Uppermill.

In Dobcross Village the road curves round to the left and then shortly after there is a post and telephone box on the right. Take this turning 'Ladcastle Road'. There is no space to park a car on Ladcastle Road, without blocking golf course exits or passing places. It would be best to park near the phone box and walk up the road to the location. The grass area is denoted by two stone pillars at the side of the road.

4) #1 6201 crosses the viaduct with a 'Cotton Mills' charter as it heads towards Manchester.
Photo by Joan Green, July, 20:15, 50mm

Dobcross

Location Notes
Two footbridges and adjoining paths to the east of the line.

1) With the rear of the train passing bridge #, 60046 runs through the valley taking the loaded bins north to Roxby.
Photo by Neil Harvey, February, 11:30, 50mm

Public Transport
Greater Manchester PTE, Services 353 and 354, run from Stalybridge Station to stops opposite the 'Navigation Inn' close to the southern bridge.

Amenities
The 'Navigation Inn' is close to the southern foot bridge. Diggle has a few pubs and takeaways.

Accommodation
There is a range of guest houses and B&Bs in both Diggle and Uppermill.

Photographic Notes
The southern foot bridge #1 offers a good view of southbound workings on line up until the early afternoon when the sun comes round to the west of the line and the bushes throw the line into shadow. Bridge #2 offers views of northbound workings in the early morning or late afternoon/early evening.

The fields to the east of the line offer a range of heights and will be 'on' from first thing in the morning until the early afternoon. The shots from the fields to the west of the line are looking up and are marred by lineside bushes.

2) 185122 heads for Newcastle.
Photo by David Dawson, March, 10:45, 35mm

3) #2 6201 heads north past the locks.
Photo by Robert Green, July, 08:15, 75mm

Dobcross

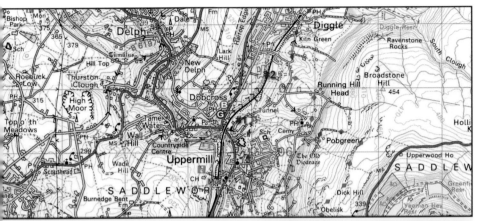

Postcode: OL3 5QR   Lat N53:33:22   Long W02:00:18

Road Directions

From the M62, Junction 22: Exit south towards Saddleworth and follow the A672 for about 3 miles to Denshaw. When you reach the 'Junction Inn', on your right, in Denshaw turn left and then right following the brown tourist sign down Delph Road. Once in Delph go straight across the staggered cross roads and follow the road into Uppermill. At the mini roundabout turn left and continue up the road. You will see a small 'Turning Circle' on the right, the footpath to #1 is off the cobbled path from this. There are road side spaces to park here. Continuing up the road there is a right spur off the road, towards Diggle. On this road, opposite Ambrose Crescent, is the public footpath to reach #2.

4) #1 60018 hauls empty binliner containers south under the footbridge while shifting them back to Northenden.
   Photo by Chris Thorp, October, 13:15, 90mm

Marsden

Location Notes

Wide views over the valley where the railway, and Huddersfield Narrow Canal, emerge from the Standedge tunnels.

1) #2 Taken from the A62. 66608 departs from the loop and enters Standedge tunnel with coal empties.
Photo by Paul Bigland, September, 16:15, 50mm

Public Transport

Marsden Station is served by Northern trains between Manchester Victoria and Huddersfield. Alternatively First's 'Purple Line', Services 182/183/185/185, run between Huddersfield Bus Station and Marsden.

Amenities

The Tunnel End Cottages have a cafe and are opposite the picnic area where you can view the railway.

Accommodation

There are a number of Hotels and Guest Houses in Marsden, but these can be busy in the summer months with tourists.

Photographic Notes

There is a spectacular early morning shot from the north of the line of trains exiting the tunnel. By lunchtime the sun will have come round for the shot from above the tunnel mouth and then for southbound trains from around the Museum area. The higher tunnel vantage point is roadside, but the rest of the area is quiet in open countryside so would suit videographers.

2) 66608 waits in the loop for a path south.
Photo by Paul Bigland, September, 16:00, 200mm

Marsden

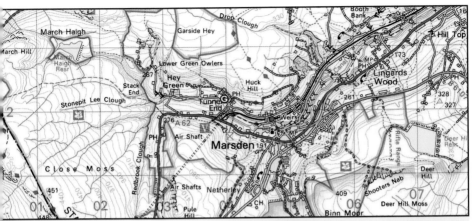

Postcode: HD7 6NH **Lat N53:36:15** **Long W01:56:23**

Road Directions

From the M62, Junction 22: Exit south towards Saddleworth and follow the A672 for about 3 miles to Denshaw. When you reach the 'Junction Inn', on your right, in Denshaw turn left and then right following the brown tourist sign down Delph Road. Once in Delph turn left at the junction onto the A62 and follow the signs towards Huddersfield. You will climb over Standedge Moor and back down again. Coming down the hill the road curves sharply to the right on the outskirts of Marsden. Shortly after this you will see a brown tourist sign to Standedge Canal Visitor Centre, and the railway down on the left (#2). Continue into the village and, just after the speed camera, turn left following the signs for the station. The best place to park is at the railway station. Once parked continue over the railway bridge and immediately turn left onto Reddisher Road which will lead to the location, or for a more pleasant walk use the canal towpath

3) 56078 emerges from 3 miles and 60 yards of Standedge darkness with the farewell charter to York.
Photo by Albert Dawson, March, 15:00, 60mm

Wellhouse, Golcar

Location Notes

A wide footpath bridge on the edge of the hill down the to Colne River Valley

1) 67021 travels east with the Northern Belle towards Huddersfield.
Photo by Neil Harvey, November, 10:15:, 100mm

Public Transport

First Calderdale and Huddersfield, Service 185, operates between Peel Street in Huddersfield and Hoyle Ing from where it would be about a 15 minute walk to the location.
Alternatively Slaithwaite is well served by the Manchester Victoria to Huddersfield Northern Trains service The station would be about 30 minutes walk away.

Amenities

There is nothing at the location, but Huddersfield is a couple of miles to the north.

Accommodation

There is nothing in the immediate area, but Huddersfield has a range of hotels and guest houses including a Travel Inn on the M62 about 4 miles away.

Photographic Notes

The bridge offers views in both directions. The parapets are not high so a step ladder is not required. The bridge is very wide so there is be plenty of room to set up video tripods and most of the noise in the area is muffled by the trees, making it ideal for videographers. However, it is more of a footpath with a large garden of weeds on either side so be prepared to do some trampling to get to the edges and to get wet if it has been raining.
The trees on the southern side of the line will cast shadows for much of the day, making the location better lit in the middle of the day when the sun is high in the sky.

Wellhouse, Golcar

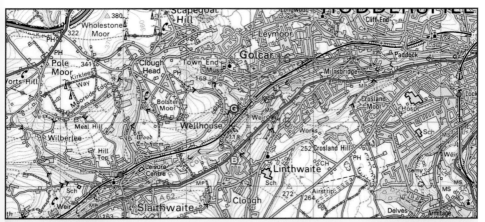

Postcode: HD7 4EN   **Lat N53:37:57**   **Long W01:51:09**

Road Directions

From the M62, Junction 23: Exit the motorway and take the A640 toward Rochdale. After about a mile turn left towards Scapegoat Hill and Golcar and go back across the M62. At the top of a hill there is a right hand bend, take the second left turn down School Lane. Go straight across at the crossroads opposite the 'Scape House Inn' and then at the bottom turn right. Take the turning signed to Bolster Moor, onto Slades Road. Half a mile later, opposite a church, turn left down the hill into Lower Wellhouse. Just before the school turn left down the rather steep Low Westwood Lane. When the road curves to the right there is a public footpath over the wall. Park around here, good hand brake or car in gear required, and follow the footpath past the houses to the bridge.

2) In full monsoon conditions, D1015 is almost at wet as the photographer as she heads west towards Buxton.
   Photo by Neil Harvey, March,11:30, 80mm

Paddock Cutting, Huddersfield

Location Notes
A footbridge over the line in a long stone walled cutting just south of Huddersfield.

1) 60045 brushes past the trees with the northbound binliner, seemingly the only freight on the line!
Photo by Nigel Cockburn, June, 12:00, 60mm

Public Transport
First Calderdale and Huddersfield, Service 302, and Team Deck, Service 302A, operate from Huddersfield Bus Station and call at Church Street to the north of the location.

Amenities
To the north of the location is a 'high street' with cafes, newsagents, and take-aways.

Accommodation
There is the Griffin Lodge Bed and Breakfast close to where the Barnsely Line crosses the A62.

Photographic Notes
The main bridge is a former road bridge, where the road has been severed to stop it being used as a cut through. The bridge sides are over seven feet high here so a step ladder is essential to see over the top. Also care is required, given the slanted angle of the bridge. The cutting runs roughly east to west so there will be options for most of the day. But given that it is a cutting,

2) 60052 and the bins viewed from Church Street.
Photo by Julie Knowles, August, 11:30, 70mm

the best time of day will be just before or after lunch when the sun is higher in the sky. The high sides to the bridge would make videoing with tripods virtually impossible.

Paddock Cutting, Huddersfield

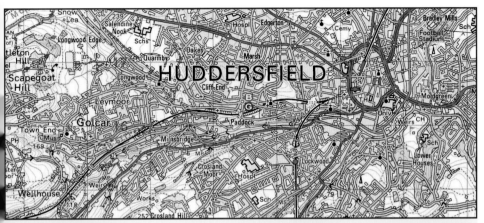

Postcode: HD1 4UF   **Lat N53:38:31**   **Long W01:48:48**

Road Directions

From the M62, Junction 24: Take the A629 into Huddersfield. After about 1½ miles there is a pedestrian crossing with lights. Immediately before this, turn right onto Luther Place. At the end of the road turn left and at the roundabout take the third exit (Gledholt Road) towards Gledholt. After passing under the railway turn right at the T-junction into Market Street. Just past the first set of shops is a turning on the left, Brow Road. Follow this to the location. There is plenty of parking at the end of the dead end road.

3) With the church of Church Street in the background, 60042 heads south to Manchester to collect more rubbish.
   Photo by Nigel Cockburn, April, 11:45, 90mm

Bradley Junction, Deighton

Location Notes
A road bridge above Bradley Junction where the main line to Mirfield and Leeds splits with a little used single track towards Brighouse and on to Hebden Bridge.

1) 60043 shivers along with an empty Stourton to Peak Forest Stone train.
Photo by Tim Ward, March, 08:00, 60mm

Public Transport
Deighton station is about a mile to the south and roughly a 20 minute walk away. Arriva Yorkshire, Service 229, operates between Huddersfield and Leeds Bus Stations and passes Deighton Station. There is a listed stop on Bridge Road with others unlisted closer to the bridge.

Amenities
Marstons Chicken shop and a cafe are at the A62/A6107 junction.

Accommodation
There is a Travelodge on the A62 about ½ mile to the south.

2) 57601 forms the tail of a charter on the single line to Brighouse.
Photo by John Rinder, December, 11:00, 130mm

Photographic Notes
This is a narrow single track road bridge leading to some industrial units to the east of the line. There is a pavement on either side of the road so it is safe to stand. The bridge sides are reasonably high so a step ladder, while not essential, would be an advantage. The point work will indicate if a train is using the single track side of the triangle towards Brighouse but you will need a long lens, or binoculars, to see how the points are set on the main line.

Bradley Junction, Deighton

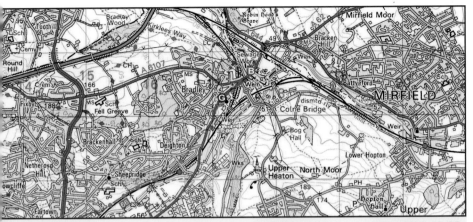

Postcode: HD2 1UU **Lat N01:44:23** **Long W53:40:37**

Road Directions

From the M62, Junction 25: Take the A644 south towards Dewsbury for about a mile. At the junction keep in the right hand lane and take the second exit onto the A62 towards Huddersfield. After about a mile, just after the 'Woodman Inn' take the left turn onto Station Road. Continue down this road and park by the church. The bridge is a short distance further on.

(3) 185135 speeds an early morning Trans-Pennine working towards Mirfield while working to Middlesborough.
July 07:30, 55mm

Mirfield

Location Notes

A footpath next to the line with a bank overlooking Heaton Lodge Junction.

1) 67002 leads an evening Birkenhead to Doncaster unit move eastward.
Photo by Pauline McKenna, June, 19:30, 105mm

Public Transport

Mirfield Station is served by Northern Trains from Manchester, Leeds, Huddersfield and Wakefield.

Amenities

Mirfield High Street has a selection of shops, newsagents and cafes.

Accommodation

There is a Travelodge at the junction of the A644/ A62/A638.

Photographic Notes

The eastern shot used to be a bridge across the line but a new housing development on the other side means this bridge has been closed and allegedly, is due for removal. This should not affect the shots as shown here as they are all from the southern side of the line. Further to the north-west there is a shot of workings coming off the Manchester line at Heaton Lodge Junction. This is easily reachable from the foot path as there is a well trodden path up the hill to the location. It is also under some overhead power lines making it easy to spot. Both locations are better suited to Leeds bound workings from mid-morning to mid-afternoon when the sun is in the south east. After that it will come round for westbound workings. The area is quiet and open so well suited for videographers.

2) 67018 heads west with the 'Northern Belle'.
Photo by Pauline Mckenna, June, 18:45, 105mm

3) 56078 heads west at Heaton Lodge.
Photo by Albert Dawson, March, 13:30, 90mm

Mirfield

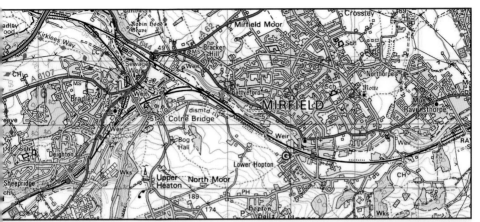

Postcode: WF14 8PN   Lat N53:40:39   Long W01:42:44

Road Directions

From the M62, Junction 25: Follow the A644 south towards Dewsbury. Once in Mirfield, after passing the speed camera on the left, you will enter the town. Just after a pedestrian crossing with lights, take the right turn signed to Hopton. Go down this road, passing under the railway and follow the road round to the right over the river, then turn right passing a play area on your left down Chadwick Lane. Take the next right and park. From here walk down the footpath to the locations.

4) 70004 lifts an east-bound Crewe Basford Hall to Hunslet wagon move up to Heaton Lodge Junction.
Photo by Mark Allatt, April, 16:45, 90mm

Ravensthorpe

Location Notes

This is a wide road bridge where the lines to Wakefield, via Healey Mills or Leeds separate.

1) 60075 shifts another load of rubbish to the Roxby waste recycling centre.
   Photo by Nigel Cockburn, July, 12:00, 100mm

Public Transport

Ravensthope station is a few minutes walk away and is well served by Northern's Leeds to Huddersfield trains.

Amenities

There is a selection of shops and cafes on Ravensthorpe high street, about 5-10 minutes walk.

Accommodation

There are a few hotels situated on the A644 running through the town.

2) 67003 with a west-bound 'Northern Belle'.
   Photo by Mark Allatt, May, 19:30, 105mm

Photographic Notes

Eastbound workings are well lit from the early morning as the line runs roughly south-west to north-east. In the late morning the sun comes round for westbounds. There is a large pipe structure on the eastern side of the bridge that would obstruct wide angle shots, a moderate zoom will get you over this.

The bridge is low sided, so a step ladder is not required. It is on a busy road and although concrete in construction, it does vibrate with passing traffic making it unsuitable for videographers.

3) 37087 & 676 work a Carlisle to Wolverhampton tour.
   Photo by Pauline McKenna, August, 20:30, 125mm

Ravensthorpe

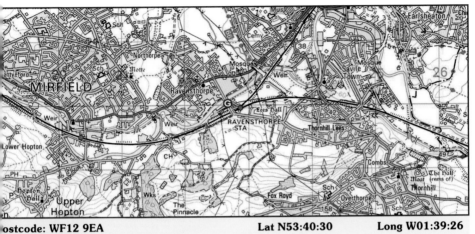

ostcode: WF12 9EA   **Lat N53:40:30**   **Long W01:39:26**

Road Directions

From the M62, Junction 25: Follow the A644 towards Dewsbury. In Ravensthorpe follow the signs for the station. You will cross over a river bridge and arrive at the station on your left. The bridge is just past the station turning. Park somewhere before the station on the main road.

4) 185105 on a Trans-Pennine Middlesbrough service provides a break from the bins.
July, 09:30, 90mm

Dewsbury Viaduct

Location Notes

A set of locations surrounding the viaduct to the north of Dewsbury Station.

1)#2 67027 leads a Serco coach collection north off the viaduct. A Stockport to York working.
Photo by Mark Allatt, May, 11:15, 80mm

Public Transport

Dewsbury station is served by both Northern and First Trans Pennine with services from Manchester, Leeds, Huddersfield, Newcastle and Middlesborough.

Amenities

There is a small newsagents at the bottom of Calums Wood Road.

Accommodation

There is the Crackenedge Guest House at the bottom of Calums Wood Road.

Photographic Notes

There are a few vantage points all of which are best suited to early mornings when the sun is to the north. #1 is the northern station car park and it also offers views of southbound workings from mid morning. #2 is a wall overlooking the line on the northern side of the viaduct. #3 is taken from Calums Wood Road through gaps in the trees. #2 can be tricky to get to, especially after wet weather as it is accessed by negotiating a copse of trees and a small bank next to the former Crackenedge Tunnel vent shaft.

2) #1 47815 with a Runcorn to Edinburgh charter.
Photo by Mark Allatt, June, 06:00, 85mm

3) #1 60080 heads away with stone bound for Stourton.
Photo by Mark Allatt, June, 06:00, 85mm

Dewsbury Viaduct

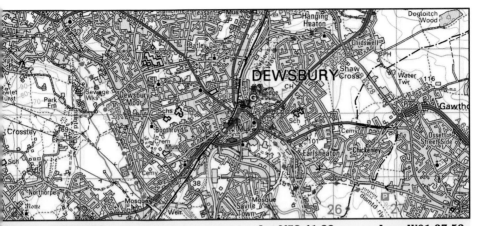

Postcode: WF13 1RF   **Lat N53:41:39**   **Long W01:37:52**

Road Directions

From the M62, Junction 25: Follow the A644 south towards Dewsbury. When you go under the railway turn left and follow the ring road round past the station. Stay in the centre lane and continue across all the traffic lights. Keep left and take the next left turn, off the ring road.

From the M1, junction 40: Take the A638 towards Dewsbury. On the ring road make a right turn, using the feeder lane, just before the factory with a chimney on the right.

At the crossroads turn left and follow this road. You will see a tunnel ventilation shaft, from the disused Crackenedge Tunnel, and further up on the right after the corner shop is the turning on to Calums Wood Road. Either park by the turning or Calums Wood Road.

4) #3 Taken from Caulms Wood Road. 60003 crosses the viaduct early in the morning.
Photo by Neil Harvey, February, 06:00, 130mm

Union Mills Viaduct, Batley

Location Notes
A collection of vantage points on either side of the Union Mills viaduct.

1) #2, 66054 on a southbound engineers working.
Photo by Mark Allatt, March, 14:45, 70mm

Public Transport
Batley Station is served by Northern trains from Manchester and Huddersfield.

Accommodation
There are a few small guest houses in Batley, but for a wider range it would be best to head to Leeds.

Photographic Notes
The main view. #1, over the viaduct is taken from open grassland to the north of Batley and offers a landscape view over the towns of Batley and Dewsbury from the north west. Although a good distance from the subject it would suit panoramic video shots. #2 is from the line side fence and is accessed by climbing a steep bank and leaning on the fence. This would be difficult to reach in wet weather as it's positioning makes it suitable only for the more adventurous photographer or videographer. #3 is a southbound shot from the eastern side of the line and would well suit morning trains heading south. You stand on the northern approach road to the station. Tall lorries, which use the road from time to time, could block your shot.

2) #3, CrossCountry HST stock heads south towards Manchester.
Photo by Mark Allatt, May, 20:30, 50mm

3) The Grid finale heads for Manchester across the viaduct.
Photo by Mark Allatt, March, 12:15, 130mm

Union Mills Viaduct, Batley

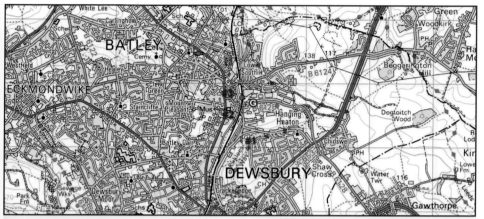

Postcode: WF17 6ER **Lat N53:42:30** **Long W01:37:23**

Road Directions

From the M62, Junction 25: Follow the A644 towards Dewsbury. When you go under the railway turn left and follow the ring road round past the station.

From the M1, junction 40: Take the A638 towards Dewsbury. Join the ring road in a clockwise direction and follow the signs to the railway station.

Pass Dewsbury railway station and stay in the centre lane at the traffic lights. Take the turning at the second set of traffic lights onto the A652, under the viaduct, towards Batley. Opposite a large white 'Legends' pub turn right up the one way street and you will see the viaduct on your right. At the mini roundabout take the either the first exit (left) to head up to the station for #2 or the third exit (right) up Mill Lane and then right on to Wood Lane, by the school and then right onto Commonside. Park on Commonside and walk up Nursery Wood Road to reach the grasslands for shot #1.

4) #1, 43357 and 378 work CrossCountry empties north across the viaduct.
Photo by Mark Allatt, May, 07:00, 70mm

Howley Park Crossing

Location Notes

Two foot crossings and a footbridge just south of the Morley Tunnel portal.

1) 185112 south-bound from Leeds while heading for Manchester Airport.
Photo by Mark Allatt, February, 16:00, 100mm

Public Transport

Arriva Yorkshire, Service 221, runs between Huddersfield and Leeds Bus Station and calls at Scotchman Lane from where it is a 5 minute walk to the location.

Batley station is about a mile to the south of the location and is about a 20-30 minute walk via footpaths to the east of the line.

Amenities

There is the 'Needless Inn' on Scotchman Lane. Otherwise there is an Aldi supermarket and some other shops on the corner of the A652 and B6123.

2) 47786, also heading south, away from the camera.
Photo by Mark Allatt, February, 14:00, 70mm

Accommodation

There is a 'Travel Inn' opposite Junction 27 of the M62.

Photographic Notes

The footbridge offers a view on the sweeping curve in both the north and south directions. The sides are reasonably high but the ends where you shoot from are low so a step ladder is not required. During the summer the trees will encroach on the shots.

The foot crossing offers a view of northbound trains sweeping in but will require the use of a medium telephoto to crop out some trackside boxes.

The locations are free from obtrusive noise and would be will suitable for videographers.

Howley Park Crossing

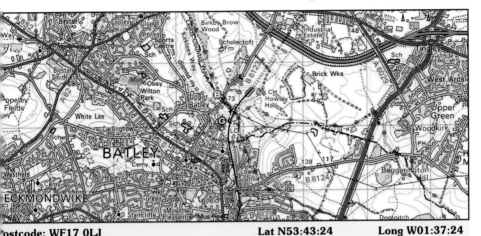

Postcode: WF17 0LJ   **Lat N53:43:24**   **Long W01:37:24**

Road Directions

From the M62, Junction 27: Follow the A650 south towards Wakefield for about a mile and then take the B6123 towards Batley for another mile. Shortly after the 'Welcome to Batley' signs at the bottom of the hill is a left turn signed as the B6123 to Batley. Take this road and turn left, opposite Blenheim House, onto York Road. Just as York Road bears round to the right there is a left turn, onto Sunnybank Road. Park at the end of this road and continue down the dirt track and the footpath will take you to the bridge. From here you can continue round past the houses and up the field to reach the farm occupation crossing.

3) 47804 works a Doncaster to Carnforth charter south under the footbridge. The back of the train is on the foot crossing.
Photo by Mark Allatt, February, 14:00, 70mm

Churwell

Location Notes
Wide open fields and foot crossings to the south of Leeds.

1) 60003 catches the rising sun on an early morning Peak Forest to Stourton working.
Photo by Mark Allatt, June, 06:00, 80mm

Public Transport
Morley station is well served by Northern Trains from Leeds and is perhaps an easier walk than that from the White Rose Centre, but parking is not as easy. From the station head out and back over the line and head south through the industrial units. At the end of the road the footpath leads to the southern crossing. There are also numerous buses from Leeds City Centre to the shopping complex.

Amenities
The White Rose Centre has pretty much anything you would need. Morley town also has a range of shops, but both are a good 20 minutes walk away.

Accommodation
There are a few B&Bs on the A653 otherwise Leeds has plenty of options.

Photographic Notes
This location offers three distinct views of the line. To the north there is a foot crossing for early morning or evening northbound shots. This will include the spire of Morley church on the top of the hill. There are also shots of southbound workings in the middle of the day

2) 31454 heads south with a saloon..
Photo by Mark Allatt, May, 12:15, 80mm

coming round the cutting. For shots during the afternoon there is a wide shot of trains sweeping round the curve southbound towards Dewsbury which would be best suited to around 13:00 when the sun will not quite have moved head-on. There is also a second foot crossing with better angles for later in the day. All the crossings are set back from the track and the northern one has slopes on both sides offering height differences to the track. The area has a constant distant hum of traffic and general 'urbanness' but it should not interfere with audio sound tracks, making the location ideal for videographers.

Churwell

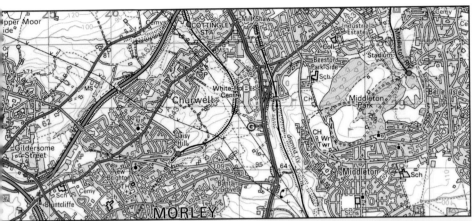

Postcode: LS11 8LL   **Lat N53:45:22**   **Long W01:34:39**

Road Directions

From the M621, Junction 1: Follow the signs for the 'White Rose Centre'. After passing the three glass sided buildings take the roundabout into the White Rose Centre and follow the black and white bus signs to the rear of the centre. Just past the bus and coach parking is the entrance to car park number 5 and opposite this is the footpath. Park in the car park and follow the footpath left and you will reach the foot crossing, or continue along the path to reach the other end of the curve and the other crossing.

3) 55022 accelerates at the start of the long climb into the Pennines with a Sheffield to Crewe charter.
Photo by Mark Allatt, August, 15:15, 115mm

Halifax and Bradford

General Notes

Another of the routes from Manchester to Leeds. This line is odd, in that it's not continuous; all trains need to reverse at Bradford Interchange. There are some tunnels and a few gradients, including the steep climb of Salterhebble bank from Greetland Junction to Dryclough Junction.

Passenger Traffic

Northern units predominate, travelling to destinations such as Leeds, York, Rochdale and Blackpool North. The staple motive power is Class 158, but 155s, 156s and 150s can appear occasionally.

1) 158759 heads towards Halifax.
July, 15:00, 130mm

Freight Traffic

There is no freight traffic booked to use the route, nor is it likely to be used for diversions.

Occasional Traffic

Bradford is a fairly popular destination with railtour promoters, but their trains have to run in 'top & tail' mode as there is no facility for locos to run-round full-length trains. Halifax is another popular charter destination. Serco test trains occasionally visit the line, but the Class 150 Sprinter unit is the usual provider. RHTT traffic has recently been operated by DRS traction based at York. traction based at York.

2) 67005 brings the Royal Train south from Halifax.
Photo by Neil Harvey, February, 40mm

3) 31602 leads 31454 out of the station on a circular test train to Forster Square.
Photo by Neil Harvey, March, 10:30, 35mm

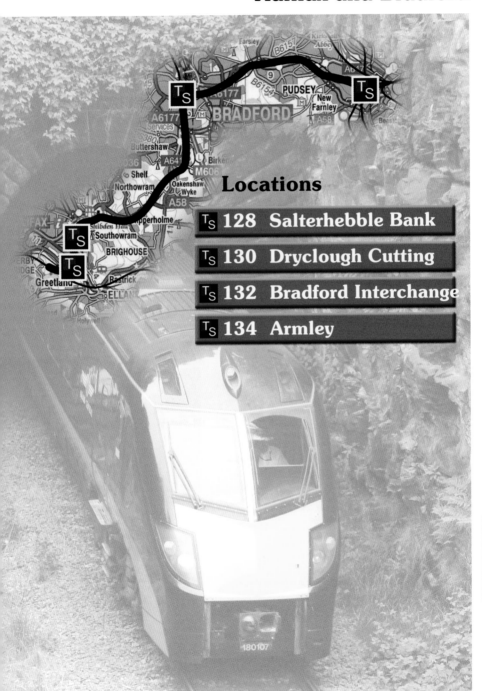

Locations

Salterhebble Bank

Location Notes
A small road bridge over the lines to Brighouse and Hebden Bridge. The Salterhebble Tunnel is one of the shortest on the network at 91 yards or 83 metres.

1) 180107 emerges from the tunnel with a Grand Central service to Bradford.
   Photo by Roger Sutcliffe, June, 12:45, 55mm

Public Transport
Halifax station is about 1¼ miles to the north and would be about a 25 minute walk. Alternatively, the location is next to the Royal Calderdale Hospital and Services 503, 536,537, 538 pass the location. They originate at Halifax Bus Station and end at Huddersfield Bus Station.

Amenities
There is small cafe and coffee shop on the main road and a petrol station and McDonalds to the south.

Accommodation
There is the 'Kirk Lea' Guest house on the Huddersfield Road or a Travel Inn a little further south.

2) 158759 with a Manchester to Bradford train.
   July, 15:00, 35mm

Photographic Notes
Salterhebble Tunnel is on the steep section of line from Greetland up to Dryclough Junction. If you are quick you will notice the tunnel going dark when a train enters and catch it, but you do need good reactions. Looking north the line on the east is climbing, towards Hebden Bridge and the western line descends towards Brighouse. You can also walk down Haigh Lane for an alternative shot. The bridge is quite narrow but sparsely used so the area is quiet. You could set up a video tripod, but you might need to move it.

3) 40145 heads south with a charter.
   Photo by Neil Harvey, September, 16:00:, 24mm

Salterhebble Bank

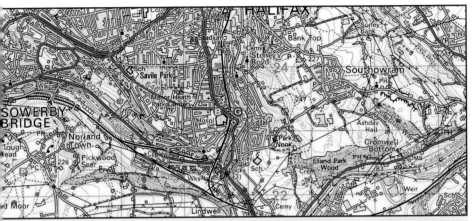

| Postcode: HX3 0PL | Lat N53:42:22 | Long W01:51:15 |

Road Directions

From the M62, Junction 24: Follow the A629 north into Halifax. After passing a McDonnalds on your right and then immediately after going over the railway line and traffic lights take the right turn, using a small filter lane than takes you over the last bit of the dual carriage way and drops you down Westbourne Crescent and the bridge. Park before the railway, as there is little room to park on the other side of the bridge.

1) 180107 drops down towards Greetland Junction with the afternoon Grand Central train to London.
Photo by Julie Knowles, June, 15:45, 55mm

Dryclough Cutting

Location Notes

Two bridges, at either end of a long cutting, over the line just to the north of Dryclough Junction where the line splits towards either Brighouse or Hebden Bridge.

1) #1 158756 drops down to Dryclough Junction while heading for Bradford Interchange.
Photo by Paul Bigland, March, 14:00, 260mm (inset)

Public Transport

Halifax station is about a mile to the north and is about a 20 minute walk to the location. Alternatively, buses that pass the Royal Calderdale Hospital, Services 503, 536,537, 538, will also pass the location. They originate at Halifax Bus Station and end at Huddersfield Bus Station. You should alight at either the Lime Avenue or Heath Lane stops.

Amenities

There is small cafe and coffee shop on the Huddersfield Road near the location and a Petrol Station and McDonalds further to the south.

Accommodation

There is the 'Kirk Lea' Guest house on the Huddersfield Road, just to the south of the location. Or a Travel Inn a little further south.

Photographic Notes

Obtaining a sunny picture will always be a problem. The sun should be straight down the cutting for an hour or so before 12.00, anytime other than that the area will be in general shade for southbound workings. For northbound workings the location will be backlit.

2) #2 158853 heads south.
Photo by Paul Bigland, March, 13:30, 240mm

The southern bridge is a footbridge, the northern is a residential road bridge. Neither require a step ladder and both are quiet and would suit videographers.

Dryclough Cutting

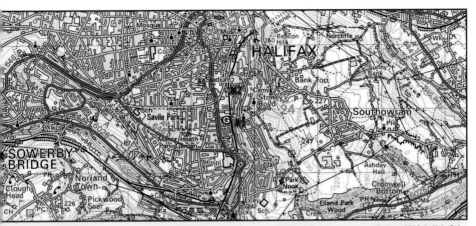

ostcode: HX3 0DE   **Lat N53:42:41**   **Long W01:51:21**

oad Directions

rom the M62, Junction 24: Follow the A629 into Halifax. After passing a McDonalds on your right
nd then going over the railway line, go up the hill and after three more sets of lights, at crossings and
nctions, turn right, opposite the speed camera, down Coronation Road. Then turn left onto any of the
obbled side streets and park considerately, at the far end. Mansion Lane is at the end of all of these roads
nd you turn right to walk down to the footbridge. Bridge #2 is about 5 minutes walk to the left, on Shaw
ane to the east of the line.

3)#1 155344 going south with a Manchester Victoria working. Bridge (#2) is visible in the background.
July, 14:45, 35mm

Mill Lane Junction, Bradford Interchange

Location Notes

A road bridge over the mouth of Bradford Interchange Station. This is the junction where the lines diverge to either Halifax or Leeds.

1) 180107 arrives at journey's end at Bradford Interchange with the evening working from King's Cross.
Photo by Julie Knowles, April, 17:30, 100mm

Public Transport

Bradford Interchange is few minutes walk from the bridge and is served by Northern Trains from places like Blackpool, Rochdale and Leeds as well as Grand Central trains from London.

Amenities

There is a small group of take-aways and a post office at the eastern end of Caledonia Street.

Accommodation

Just outside Interchange station is, on the left, a Holiday Inn and on the right, the Bradford Hilton.

Photographic Notes

The station is bordered, to the east, by a large retaining wall, this will throw shadows across the line for a good part of the morning, but after

2) 31459 on the tail of a Bradford Forster Square test train.
Photo by Neil Harvey, March, 11:00, 75mm

about 11.00 the light should be on until late afternoon for departures. Looking to the south the lines diverge with the Leeds lines heading off to the left and the Halifax lines continuing straight on. The bridge sides are quite high so a step ladder, while not essential, would be helpful.

The area has a general city 'hum' about it but should not be too much of a problem for audio. The bridge sides however, would make video difficult without a tall tripod.

Mill Lane Junction, Bradford Interchange

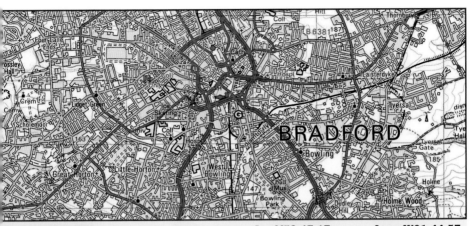

stcode: BD4 7BQ **Lat N53:47:17** **Long W01:44:57**

oad Directions

om the M606, Junction 3: Follow the ring road (A6177) east following the signs for the city centre. Cross
e roundabout and at the next turn left and drive down onto the A650 towards Keighley. Cross two more
undabouts, still heading towards Keighley, and just after a lay-by and before a large overhead road sign
rn left into Hall Lane and then, opposite the little row of shops, turn right onto Caledonia Street. There
e lots of double yellow lines but you should be able to find somewhere to park off the road and walk the
st few metres to the bridge.

) 180114 snakes into Interchange on its initial test run from Heaton depot
Photo by Paul Bigland, April, 13:45, 70mm

Heights Lane, Armley

Location Notes

A road bridge over the line in a housing estate in the Armley district of Leeds.

1) 158888, a long way from home while on hire to Northern, heads for Huddersfield via Bradford.
Photo by Lee Marshall, March, 14:15, 55mm

Public Transport

First Leeds, Service 16, operates at frequent intervals from a stop in Wellington Street near Leeds Central Railway station and calls at the top of Heights Lane. First Leeds, Service 5, runs every 10 minutes from the station and calls on Heights Drive just to the south of the location.

Amenities

There is a row of shops on Heights Drive, about a 5 minute walk to the location. Head south from the bridge, turn right on Heights Way, there is a path through the houses and then right again on Heights Drive.

Accommodation

There is nothing in the immediate area, but Leeds city centre is about 2 miles to the east and has a broad range of Hotels, Guest Houses and B&Bs. These include an Ibis and Travel Inn where the A58(M) becomes the A58.

Photographic Notes

The line runs east to west at the location but curves in from the north for workings heading towards Leeds. This should give you angle options for any time of the day. Both sides of the bridge are around seven feet high so a step ladder will be required. The eastern side of the bridge has a pavement, but the western side does not have one along the full length, in the corner the pavement ends and you could use a step ladder here. There is also a palisade fence which you will need to shoot through. The more adventurous photographer may choose to stand on the wall and shoot over this.

Heights Lane, Armley

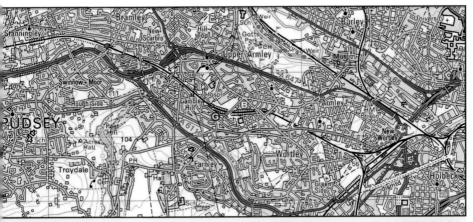

Postcode: LS12 3SP   **Lat N53:47:46**   **Long W01:36:31**

Road Directions

From the M621, Junction 2: Exit north onto the A643 towards Wetherby. Follow this road north for half a mile and after passing under two bridges, take the left exit, signed towards Wortley. At the end of the road turn right and then left and follow the road round. You will go under three railway bridges and then come to a T-junction by the Crown Hotel on Tong Road. Turn left and continue for a mile. At the traffic lights keep in the right hand lane and bear right onto Whingate for another ½ mile. A road joins from the right, opposite a park and just after this is the left turn onto Heights Lane. Continue down the road and park on the other side of the bridge.

) 158756 speeds around the bend with a Northern working for Leeds.
July, 12:30, 45mm

Healey Mills to Drax

General Notes

Running across the centre of the area covered by this book, the route has a mixture of traffic and geographical features. The urban sprawl of Wakefield lies at the western end, before the buildings thin out as the line reaches the small towns of Pontefract and Knottingley. The line then runs into the open countryside around Hensall and Snaith.

Passenger Traffic

Grand Central operates three trains a day in each direction with Class 180s along the route from Healey Mills to Knottingley and then to Doncaster via Askern. The Healey Mills end is used for Wakefield to Selby workings. There are also local workings from Knottingley to Leeds and Wakefield, operated by Northern 142s, 144s or 150s. East of Knottingley, a minimal service of three trains a day is operated by Northern between Leeds and Goole.

1) 142020 heads for Knottingley at Horbury.
August, 11:45, 85mm

Freight Traffic

The yard at Healey Mills is mothballed and is used only for storage or in the event of problems elsewhere. There are two 'binliners' taking Manchester's waste to Roxby on Humberside. In the Wakefield area, a stream of intermodals runs to either Europort or Stourton, Leeds. There are a few intermittent scrap flows, and wagons going for repair at either Leeds or Horbury. Gypsum flows take waste by-product from the power stations. Coal is a constant flow and, sometimes, imported 'pet coke' going to the power stations at Ferrybridge, Eggborough and Drax. All these workings are in the hands of either DB Schenker, Freightliner or GBRf. Recently bio-mass has begun flowing into Drax in modified covered wagons as this power station can now be multi-fired.

2) 66512 with a Ratcliffe to Hunslet wagon move.
Photo by Ross Beyers, June, 11:30, 60mm

Occasional Traffic

This is a popular route for charters running from Manchester to York, as it avoids Leeds. The Northern Belle also puts in the odd appearance, and there are occasional Serco test trains running on an 'as required' basis. Fly ash trains shift power station waste over the route when a project requires it.

3) 43087 on the tail of a Cotswold HST charter.
Photo by Steve Jackson, June, 11:30, 60mm

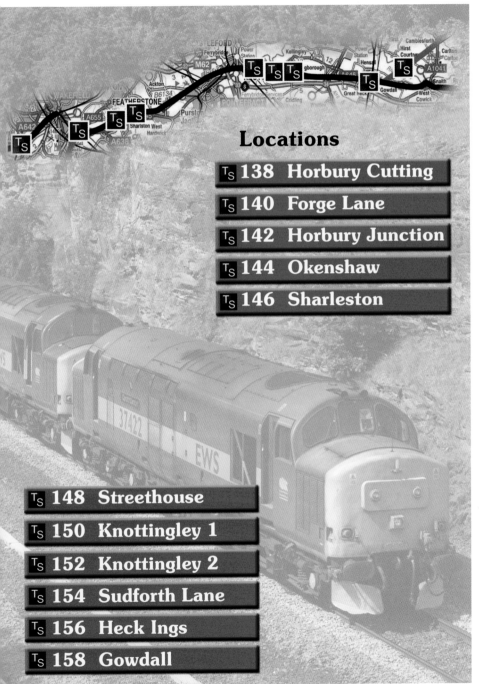

Locations

Horbury Cutting

Location Notes

A collection of road bridges over the line to the west of the mothballed Healey Mills Yard. Some carry busy main roads others are just roads connecting the A638 to parks and farms.

Public Transport

Arriva Yorkshire, Services 231/232/265, operate from Wakefield Bus Station and pass along Highfield Road before heading to separate destinations.

Amenities

There are Newsagents, The Bulls Head pub and The Quarry Inn scattered along the main road to the north of the line. There is a Chinese take-away on the other side of the line a few hundred yards walk from bridge #4.

Accommodation

The Quarry Inn on the A642 offers bed and breakfast. Alternatively, there are Travel Inns at Junction 38 of the M1 to the south.

Photographic Notes

Each bridge offers views of the line from above. A step ladder is not required at any of the bridges as they are all low sided, but it could be helpful at #5 and #3 for an easier view.

All the shots are well lit from mid-morning onwards and suit eastbound trains until mid-afternoon, after which the westbound workings will have favourable lighting. Few of the bridges offer shots from the northern side of the line.

Bridge #5 has the widest view with Healey Mills Yard being next to the bridge.

Bridge #4 is opposite the wagon repair shop which still sees occasional use.

Bridges #3 and #2 border the high sided stone cutting. Shadows can creep onto the line during the early morning between these bridges.

Bridges #1 to #3 are on quiet roads but none have wide pavements making the setting up of tripods for video tricky, but not impossible.

Bridge #4 and #5 are on main roads and traffic noise would interfere with audio recordings

1) #1 66609 heads east with a binliner.
August, 12:00, 95mm

2) #3 Class 37s shift wagons to Marcroft Engineering.
Photo by Mark Allatt, June, 12:15, 170mm

3) #4 60059 & 008 depart Healy Mills yard on a binliner.
Photo by Mark Allatt, March, 13:45, 170mm

4) #5 66090 heads west with scrap Class 56s.
Photo by Mark Allatt, July, 13:00, 55mm

Horbury Cutting

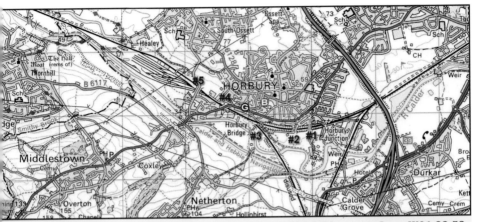

Postcode: WF4 5AS   Lat N53:39:20   Long W01:32:53

Road Directions

From the M1, Junction 40: Follow the A638 towards Wakefield for about ½ mile. Just after 'The Malt Shovel' pub take the right turn, with a brown tourist sign to the 'National Mining Museum' and follow this road along it's length. At the end turn right, still following the brown signs onto the A642 Horbury Road. This road passes all the bridges, most of which have quiet residential streets on which you can park.

5) #2 - 37422 & 410 pass under Addingford Lane with a Basford Hall to Scunthorpe wagon move.
Photo by Julie Knowles, Month, 13:15, 60mm

Forge Lane

Location Notes
A track level shot looking over a wall to the line just west of Horbury Junction.

1) 66953 slows for Horbury Junction past St. Mary's church with an eastbound binliner.
Photo by Julie Knowles, April, 12:00, 95mm

Public Transport
Arrivia Yorkshire, Service 127, operates from Wakefield Bus station and calls at Hallcroft Drive which is a 10 minute walk to the location.

Amenities
There is a sandwich shop on Mill Field Road straight on from the Forge Lane Turning. There is a newsagents on the A642 close to the bus stop.

Accommodation
The Quarry Inn on the A642 offers Bed and Breakfast. Alternatively, there are Travel Inns at Junction 38 of the M1.

2) 56071 heads a Neville Hill to Healy Mills tank move.
Photo by Mark Allatt, March, 15:00, 130mm

Photographic Notes
The line is facing south-west at this point so it will have options for east, Wakefield bound workings in the morning with the sun coming round for west, Mirfield bound workings after about 11.00. There are only positions on the southern side of the line so after about 17.00 the sun is on the wrong side. In the summer, eastbound shots are often hindered by vegetation growing in the middle of the tracks. The wall is reasonably high so a step ladder will be a required. This will also make the location difficult for all but the tallest video tripods.

Forge Lane

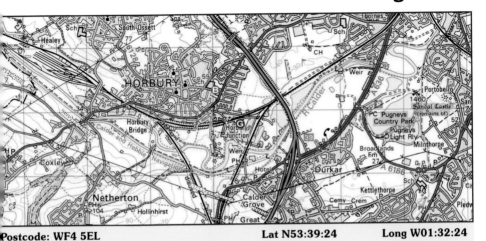

Postcode: WF4 5EL   **Lat N53:39:24**   **Long W01:32:24**

Road Directions

From the M1, Junction 40: Follow the A638 towards Wakefield for about ½ mile. Just after 'The Malt Shovel' pub take the right turn, with a brown tourist sign to the 'National Mining Museum' and follow this road along it's length. At the end turn right, still following the brown signs onto the A642 Horbury Road. Continue down the road, passing under the M1. Shortly after this take the left turn signed for 'Slazengers Sports Club' and 'St. Mary's Church'. Follow this road round and you will come to some traffic lights protecting a single lane bridge. Immediately after the bridge turn left on to Forge Lane; the location is ¼ mile down the road. Park anywhere on the roadside.

3) 47760 & 37676 head west with a Barnetby to Carnforth empty stock move.
Photo by Steve Jackson, March, 15:00, 60mm

Horbury Junction

Location Notes
A footpath running under the M1 motorway at the junction where the lines to Mirfield and Barnsley split.

1) 158790 clatters across Horbury Junction in front of the junction box while heading for Leeds.
August, 13:00, 70mm

Public Transport
Arrivia Yorkshire, Service 127, operates from Wakefield Bus station and calls at Hallcroft Drive which is a 25 minute walk to the location.

Amenities
There is a sandwich shop on Mill Field Road. Also, the 'Wood Kite' pub is situated just off the A636 in Durkar.

Accommodation
The Cedar Court Hotel is located just off Junction 39 of the M1. There is a Travel Inn on the Durkar side of the M1.

2) 180105 slows on its journey west to Bradford.
August, 13:00, 105mm

Photographic Notes
The location is based around the motorway bridge supports. To see over the fence you can clamber up onto the concrete sections. These are about 4 feet wide, but about 5 feet high, so a step ladder might be handy to get up on to them. The motorway above will provide a constant drone, but if you are under the bridge then the noise of a passing working should drown that out. There is plenty of room for tripods so this will be an interesting option for videographers.

3) 158784 heads east with a Sheffield-bound working.
August, 13:15, 60mm

Horbury Junction

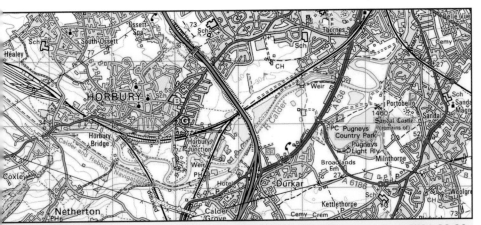

Postcode: WF4 5ED **Lat N53:39:32** **Long W01:32:00**

Road Directions

From the M1, Junction 40: Follow the A638 towards Wakefield for about ½ mile. Just after 'The Malt Shovel' pub take the right turn, with a brown tourist sign to the 'National Mining Museum' and follow this road along it's length. At the end turn right, still following the brown signs onto the A642 Horbury Road. Continue down the road, passing under the M1. Shortly after this take the left turn signed for 'Slazengers Sports Club' and 'St. Mary's Church'. Follow this road round and you will come to some traffic lights protecting a single lane bridge. Immediately after the bridge turn left on to Forge Lane and follow the road all the way to the end. You will drive under the Barnsley line and reach a dirt car park for the lakes. Park here and follow the edge of the lake round towards the M1 motorway and the location.

4) 67018 powers a Northern Belle working from Birmingham International to York.
Photo by Mark Allatt, June, 10:00, 145mm

Okenshaw

Location Notes
A small footbridge over the line, and a foot crossing over a rarely used spur to the Monk Bretton branch.

1) #2, A shiny 66152 heads east with a Wakefield to Tilbury intermodal.
   Photo by Mark Allatt, March, 15:30, 105mm

Public Transport
Arriva Yorkshire, Service 485, operates from Wakefield Bus Station and passes along the 'Doncaster Road'.

Amenities
There is Al's Cafe, formerly the Redbeck Cafe, just to the east on the main road. There is also a petrol station opposite.

Accommodation
The Redbeck Motel is just to the east. Otherwise Wakefield is a close by.

Photographic Notes
The (#1) footbridge is the main location. This is a narrow footbridge with 3 iron pipe railings so there is no need for a step ladder. On one side is a large road bridge (#2) and the other side has a signal that also indicates the route, feather for the line to Hare Park Junction and on to the East Coast Main Line or no feather for round to Crofton and on to Pontefract. This bridge carries the freight only line to Monk Bretton. This line also has a rarely used spur. The footpath on from the bridge crosses the spur and can be seen on the southern side of the road bridge. The area is quiet so would suit videographers but, given the bridge width, a tripod would be an obstruction.

2) #1 - 37612/611 head for the ECML.
   Photo by Steve Jackson, August, 15:30, 60mm

3) 37218/607 at Oakenshaw Level Crossing.
   Photo by Mark Walker, June, 12:00, 55mm

Okenshaw

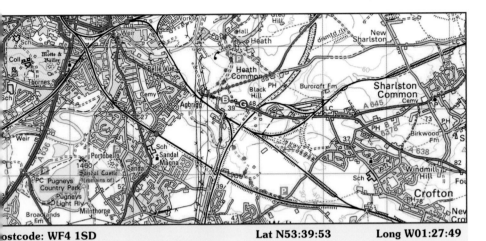

ostcode: WF4 1SD **Lat N53:39:53** **Long W01:27:49**

oad Directions

rom the M62, Junction 31: Follow the A655 towards Wakefield and cross straight over 2 small undabouts. At the third roundabout take the third exit, right, towards Wakefield. After about ½ mile you ill come to another roundabout where you should turn left towards Old Snydale. Follow this road for bout 4½ miles and you will reach some traffic lights at a junction. Keeping out of the bus lane, after the st light keep left to turn left. Once heading back up the main road the first right turn takes you over the 2) road bridge, but there is nowhere to park, so continue on for the footpath. As you drive along the road ou will notice a turning on the right. From the there is the public footpath that goes over the wall by means f stone steps. This is the path to the location. You can park on the main road in front of the houses but ou may find it better to continue over the railway and park in the residential side streets and walk back.

) #1, 37410 heads an empty long welded rail train south-east towards Pontefract under the road bridge.
Photo by Phil Wright, July, 12:45, 80mm

Sharleston, Cow Lane

Location Notes

A road over bridge, or surrounding embankments from field edges, close to the crest of gradient.

1) 180112 heads east with a London King's Cross working from Bradford Interchange.
   Photo by Ross Byers, June, 11:15, 70mm

Public Transport

Arriva Yorkshire, Service 148, operates from Wakefield Bus Station and calls at the top of Cow Lane. Streethouse Station is about 1¼ miles from the location and is served by Northern trains from Knottingley to Wakefield Kirkgate.

Amenities

Al's Cafe, formerly the Redbeck Cafe provides a good breakfast and meals. Opposite this there is a petrol station. At the junction of the B6378 and A638 there is the 'Cock and Crown' pub which also has a carvery a sandwich shop and an Indian take-away.

Accommodation

The Redbeck Motel on the A638, near Burcroft Farm, is well reviewed. Otherwise Wakefield is a few miles away with a wide range of Hotels and B&Bs to suit all pockets.

Photographic Notes

The bridge offers clean views in both directions. On all four sides of the bridge are footpaths or the edges of fields. These will allow you to look back to the bridge from the cutting sides, although trees can be a problem sometimes. The line runs roughly north-east to south-west so will be well lit at all times of the day. The road is not that busy and is mainly used by local traffic, so apart from the odd car or lorry, it should not be too noisy and would suit videographers.

Sharleston, Cow Lane

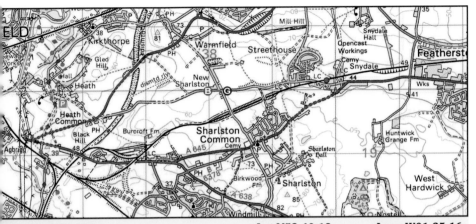

ostcode: WF4 1BD   **Lat N53:40:19**   **Long W01:25:16**

Road Directions

From the M62, Junction 31: Follow the A655 towards Wakefield and cross straight over 2 small roundabouts. At the third roundabout take the third exit, right, towards Wakefield. Follow this road for 3 miles until you reach Warmfield Village. There are bus stops on either side of the road and immediately after this turn left into Crossley Street. Continue towards Sharlston village to the T-junction where you should turn left, then immediately right onto Cow Lane.

Park on the roadside to the north of the bridge.

2) 66555 with a Drax power station to Crewe cement tanks working.
Photo by Julie Knowles, July, 12:45, 65mm

Streethouse, Gin Lane

Location Notes

A pair of foot crossings on either side of a platform of the old station, at the site of the former junction with the line to Sharlston Colliery.

1) 150276 rattles eastwards with a Wakefield Kirkgate to Knottingley shuttle service.
Photo by Mark Walker, March, 12:45, 28mm

Public Transport

Arriva Yorkshire, Services 148 and 150, operate from Wakefield Bus Station and call at opposite ends of Gin Lane. The 150 calling at the southern end, the 148 at the northern. Streethouse station is about ½ mile from the location and is served by Northern trains from Knottingley to Wakefield Kirkgate.

Amenities

There is a small post office and fish and chip shop on the main road through Streethouse.

Accommodation

The Redbeck Motel on the A638, near Burcroft Farm, is well reviewed and also has a cafe serving good fry-ups.

Photographic Notes

2) 31459 heads away, forming the tail of a test train.
Photo by Mark Walker, March, 12:30, 135mm

The crossing fences offer a close up shot of trains in either direction. Between both paths is an abandoned platform. There is a long straight heading in from Sharlston, to the west, and a slight curve in, then straight in the other direction. Eastbound workings should be well lit until late morning when the sun will come round to better suit west bound workings. The area is free from noise and has space to move around so would suit videographers.

Streethouse, Gin Lane

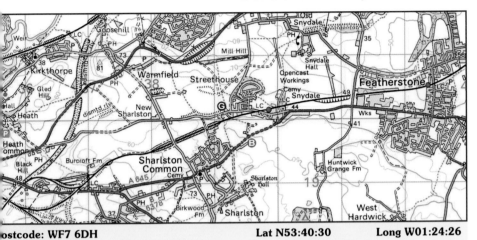

ostcode: WF7 6DH   Lat N53:40:30   Long W01:24:26

oad Directions

rom the M62, Junction 31: Follow the A655 towards Wakefield and cross straight over 2 small
oundabouts. At the third roundabout take the third exit, right, towards Wakefield. After about ½ mile you
ill come to another roundabout where you should turn left towards Old Snydale. Follow this road to the
rst right turn onto Mill Lane. Take this and continue down the road, turning right at the junction at the end.
lmost immediately after the turn are bus stops and, at the time of writing, a derelict pub.
ark on the tarmac area in front of the pub and there are two paths. Follow the one to the left down to the
cation being careful not to trip over the remains of the, disconnected, colliery branch.

3) 31602 & 459 pass through Streethouse with a Doncaster circular via Hull, Gilberdyke, Featherstone & Wakefield.
Photo by Mark Walker, March, 12:30, 70mm

Knottingley, Englands Lane

Location Notes

A footbridge over the top of a manually operated road crossing. Just to the east of the bridge is a crossover so locomotives from the depot can reverse. The left line, on the western side of the bridge is th Knottingley avoider line which heads straight to Doncaster.

1) 66080 and 144023 both face Knottingley - the 66 on empties from Drax, the 144 reversing before heading back to Leeds.
Photo by Mark Bearton, July, 11:00, 325mm

Public Transport

Knottingley has a regular train service from Leeds. Exit the station and at the main road at the top turn right. Turn right again at the traffic lights, cross the railway and take the first left past the Train Depot. Continue down this road, passing a chip shop on the left until you reach the crossing.
Arriva Services 145 and 148 pass the crossing and run about every 30 minutes from Wakefield and Pontefract to Knottingley.

Amenities

There is a small local supermarket on Spawd Bone Lane just round the corner, west of the bridge. There is also a sandwich shop at the north end of the road.

Accommodation

'The Old Dairy Farm' is just to the south on Englands Lane.

Photographic Notes

The bridge sides are lattice in construction so a step ladder is not required. The line runs roughly east to west so has options for most of the day, with the shot with Ferrybridge power station in the background being suitable until late morning.

2) From the next bridge 66623 heads to Eggborough.
July, 15:30, 85mm

Knottingley, Englands Lane

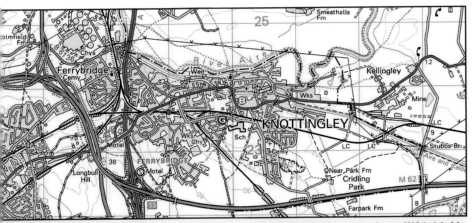

ostcode: WF11 0JB　　　Lat N53:42:24　　　Long W01:14:41

oad Directions

rom the M62, Junction 33: Turn north onto the A1 for one junction, exiting onto the A645. At the top of the
ip road, turn left, east, and into Knottingley. After you cross the railway, the station is on the right. Turn
ght at the traffic lights immediately after the station, cross the railway and take the first left. This leads you
ast Knottingley Depot and after about 500 yards brings you to Englands Lane Crossing on the left.
ark on the roadside in Spawd Bone Lane.

) 66596 heads for Eggborough power station with loaded coal wagons from Immingham docks.
Photo by Andrew Wills, November, 11:00, 115mm

Knottingley, Blackburn Lane

Location Notes

An occupational crossing in open fields to the east of Knottingley.

1) With a good old-fashioned rake of HAA hoppers in tow, 66118 heads west towards Drax.
   Photo by Mark Bearton, January, 11:15, 85mm

Public Transport

Knottingley Station is about 2 miles walk from the location. Arriva Yorkshire, Service 150, operates between Selby and Wakefield Bus Station. It stops at Knottingley Station and Weeland Road, which would be about a 20 minute walk to the location.

Amenities

The are no facilities around the crossing, however there is a range of shops, including two fish and chip shops, in Knottingley itself.

Accommodation

There is a TraveLodge off junction 33 of the M62, a Travel Inn on the A645 to the west of Knottingley and couple of smaller B&Bs in Knottingley.

Photographic Notes

The line runs roughly east to west, so the sun will be on the front of trains heading west towards Knottingley until late morning, before favouring the other direction, towards Goole. The line in the distance curves from the north-east and drops sharply from the east approaching the crossing, giving good views of westbound empty coal trains approaching.

These regularly come to a stand at the signal by the crossing which is ideal for videographers. Shots the other way are slightly restricted by lineside vegetation, though decent lineside shots are still possible.

Knottingley, Blackburn Lane

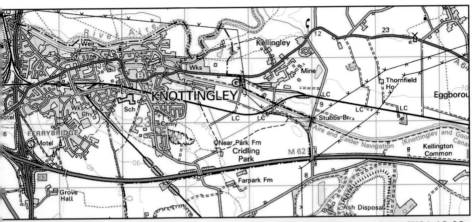

Postcode: WF11 8DA   **Lat N53:42:08**   **Long W01:13:03**

Road Directions

From the M62, Junction 33: Turn north onto the A1 for one junction then onto the A645. At the top of the slip road, turn left and follow the A645 through the town, passing both the station and the shops on the right. The road narrows between houses and near the end of the town there is a triangular junction on the right. Take this road (Common Lane) which narrows towards the factories. Continue down the road and park by the site of a demolished factory, then follow the rough farm track (Blackburn Lane) to the crossing.

2) 66719 heads west towards Knottingley after replenishing Eggborough's coal supplies.
  Photo by Adam Parkinson, April, 13:30, 105mm

Sudforth Lane

Location Notes
A level crossing with the Kellingley Colliery to the west and holding sidings to the east.

1) 66721 catches the setting winter sun as it returns empties from Drax to Tyne Dock for a refill of imported coal.
Photo by Scott Patterson, December, 14:30, 55mm

Public Transport
Arriva Yorkshire, Service 150, operates between Selby and Wakefield Bus Station. It stops at Knottingley Station and then at the top of Sudforth Lane, which would be about a 10 minute walk to the location.

Amenities
There is nothing at the location. Knottingley has a range of shops and take-aways.

Accommodation
The 'Old Post Office' guest house is in Eggborough just to the east of the location and there are a few Travel Inn style places back towards the A1 in Knottingley.

2) A collection of 66s with trains for Drax and Immingham.
Photo by Peter Bradshaw, July, 10:45, 115mm

Photographic Notes
The location is around a level crossing so there will be notice of approaching trains when the barriers go down. Looking west you have a backdrop of Kellingley colliery. To the east are holding sidings where trains can sit for hours. The area is quiet apart from a general 'clanking' from the colliery facility so would be suitable for videographers.

Sudforth Lane

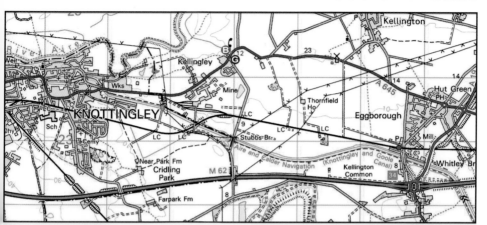

Postcode: DN14 0SZ   **Lat N53:42:15**   **Long W01:11:50**

Road Directions

From the M62, Junction 33: Turn north onto the A1 for one junction then onto the A645. At the top of the slip road, turn left and follow the road through Knottingley, passing both the station and the shops on the right. About 1½ miles after the town take the left turn into Sudforth Lane and you will reach the crossing. The road is quiet and it is possible to park on the roadsides.

Be aware that a water tanker from the colliery 'washes' the road on a regular basis.

3) 66510 with a short rake of coke wagons from Immingham heads into the sidings before continuing on to Drax.
   Photo by Scott Patterson, December, 12:30, 55mm

Heck Ings

Location Notes
A manually operated crossing close to Hensall Junction, where the branch to Drax rejoins the main line. The crossing gates are closed for road traffic between 20.00 and 08.00.

1) Blasting south along the East Coast Main Line, 43123 leads a Grand Central service for King's Cross.
Photo by Adam Parkinson, July, 14:30, 95mm

Public Transport
Hensall Station is about 30 minutes walk from the location.
Arriva Yorkshire, Service 150, operates between Selby and Wakefield Bus Station. It stops at Knottingley, Whitley Bridge and Hensall Stations and the corner of Hensall Village from where it would be a 15 minute walk to the location.

2) A First Group Hull service 180 heads north on the ECML.
July, 14:00, 95mm

Amenities
There is nothing at the location. There are a few shops and a petrol station in Snaith to the east.

Accommodation
Snaith has some small hotels and B&Bs. Goole is a few more miles to the east and has a much larger selection.

Photographic Notes
The line is just west of Hensall Junction where trains join the main line from the Drax branch. You also have a view of trains on the East Coast Main line. The line is open on both sides and has options throughout the day.
Being quiet and open the location would suit videographers, especially as trains are accelerating away from Hensall Junction.

3) 60002 powers empty HAAs away from Drax.
Photo by Neil Gibson, November, 13:00, 105mm

Heck Ings

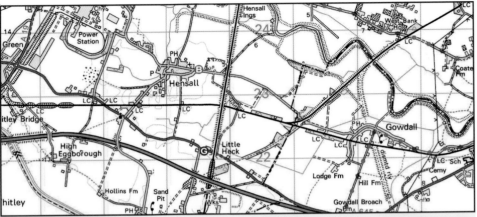

Postcode: DN14 0XD **Lat N53:41:51** **Long W01:05:27**

Road Directions

From the M62, Junction 34: Head north towards Selby on the A19 and in just under 1 mile, turn right at the first roundabout onto the A645 to Snaith for just over 2½ miles, crossing over the Goole Line. Immediately after passing under the East Coast Main Line turn left onto Little Heck Common Lane. This road leads to the crossing. There is space to park on either side of the crossing.

4) With its train still passing under the ECML, 66708 heads east towards Drax.
Photo by Scott Borthwick, October, 12:45, 65mm

Gowdall

Location Notes

An embankment close to the river Aire crossing on the former Hull and Barnsley Mainline which is now a double track branch into Drax Power station.

It's worth noting, to avoid confusion, that when driving in the area the 'main' line from Hull is a narrow, weed ridden, rusty single track and the 'branch' to Drax is a gleaming double track section.

1) 66526 brings a short set towards the power station.
Photo by Mark Bearton, March, 12:00, 325mm

Public Transport

Arriva Yorkshire, Service 150, operates between Selby and Wakefield Bus Station. It stops at Knottingley Station and the corner of Hensall Village from where it would be about an hour walk to the location.

Amenities

There is nothing at the location, Snaith has a small selection of shops.

Accommodation

Snaith has some small hotels and B&Bs. Goole is a few more miles to the east and has a much larger selection.

2) A wide view towards the river Aire.
July, 13:15, 170mm

Photographic Notes

Trains climb up a slight grade to cross the river so workings in either direction will be powering along. There are also signals protecting the power station loop and the main lines, so workings can often be paused before access to either is granted. For workings exiting Drax, the line sweeps round and crosses a large iron bridge over the river where shots can be had with the chimneys of Drax in the background. The area can often become overgrown in the summer months. The location is quiet and open so would suit videographers.

3) 66008 approaches the end of the line at Drax.
July, 12:47, 260mm

Gowdall

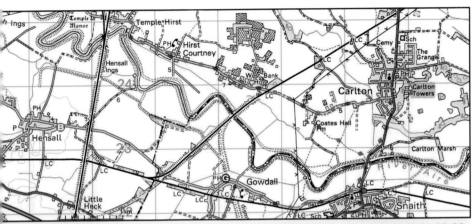

Postcode: DN14 0AJ   **Lat N53:42:16**   **Long W01:03:32**

Road Directions

From the M62, Junction 34: Follow the A19 towards Selby for about a mile and then, at the roundabout, take the A645 right towards Snaith. Continue for about 4 miles and you will be driving parallel to the M62. Take the left turn, signed towards Gowdall. You will cross over the single track line to Goole and shortly after that reach a T-junction. Turn left here passing the 'Boot and Shoe Inn' on the right. Further on the road curves to the right and just after this are the national speed limit signs. After these there is a dirt track on the right. Drive carefully up here and park.

From here continue on foot up the former track bed and you will reach the location.

4) 66727 crosses the river with empties returning to Redcar.
Photo by Neil Harvey, March, 13:30, 130mm

Further Reading...

Carry on Clagging
Preserved Traction 2010

A new full colour pocket book detailing all the preserved, former BR diesel & electrics. For each locomotive we detail all the numbers carried, current livery & location, date introduced & withdrawn, plus the date preserved. This will prove to be a very useful book for those with an interest in the preservation scene.

88 pages, 81 photos, A6 softback.

GRIDS
The Class 56 Story

Features their conception in the early 1970s to the preservation scene of today. The Grids have captured the imagination and devotion of enthusiasts nationwide. This is the complete story of their varied and unusual lives. **128 pages, 200 photos, diagrams and tables, A4 softback, Over 60,000 words.**

BRITS ABROAD

An in-depth look at the diesel and electric locos that have worked on our national network and, at some point in their lives, overseas as well. This is a fascinating subject which was long overdue for serious review. **100 pages, 200 photos, diagrams and tables, A4 softback, Over 35,000 words.**

We also produce a wide range of DVDs

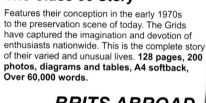

Full details can be found on our website...

www.visionsinternational.biz

^T_S Trainspots
The Series

1. Midlands

Ve still have a few copies left of *Trainspots* - Midlands. It features the ollowing lines:

Birmingham - Nuneaton	*Bedford - Bletchley*
Derby - Water Orton	*Northampton Loop*
Peterborough - Derby	*Bletchley - Birmingham*
Bedford - Leicester	*Bicester - Birmingham*

. . . .

2. East Anglia

Number 2 features the following lines:

East Suffolk & Wherry lines	*Ely to Peterborough*
North Norfolk line	*Bury St Edmunds line*
Ipswich to Sizewell & Felixstowe	*Cambridge to Kings Lynn*
Norwich to Ipswich & Ely	

. . . .

3. The North West

Number 3 features the following lines:

WCML - Warrington to Carnforth	*Bolton to Hellifield*
Sefton & West Lancs	*The Little North Western*
Manchester to Blackpool	*WCML - Carnforth to Crewe*
Preston to Todmorden	*The Cumbrian Coast*

. . . .

Coming Soon

The fifth volume of *Trainspots* covering the Northern section of Scotland is scheduled for release in February 2011.

Please check our website for details nearer the time.

Visions International
22 The Chase
Boreham
Essex CM3 3DY
tel:01245 465974
www.visionsinternational.biz

Index

The locations in this book are listed in alphabetical order with relevant page numbers. The coloured squares refer to the coloured chapter tabs.